TENACITY *WELL DIRECTED*

What else but a book to describe
our publishing history and the
pride and happiness it has brought.
A big thank-you to all coworkers
throughout the fifty years.

—HJL

TENACITY
WELL DIRECTED

THE INSIDE STORY

OF HOW A PUBLISHING HOUSE

WAS CREATED AND BECAME A

SLEEPING GIANT IN ITS FIELD—

WELL, NOT EXACTLY

HARRY LERNER

 FIRST AVENUE EDITIONS
MINNEAPOLIS ▪ NEW YORK ▪ LONDON

First Avenue Editions
241 First Avenue North
Minneapolis, MN 55401 U.S.A.

Website address: www.lernerbooks.com

Library of Congress Cataloging-in-Publication data is available.
ISBN: 978–0–7613–4075–1
Manufactured in the United States of America.
1 2 3 4 5 6 – DP – 14 13 12 11 10 09

FRONT COVER: This 1950 Renault 4CV took me through
much of Europe. The falling floorboard provided a good
view of the road.

The typewriters pictured in this book come
from my collection. Two are Underwoods, and
two are from LC Smith & Bros., which later
became Smith-Corona.

The small artworks you see sprinkled
throughout the text are illustrations taken
from our books.

TABLE OF CONTENTS

MY FATHER'S VISION of our publishing company has served us well. Through lots of hard work and a little bit of luck, he was able to publish thousands of excellent books as well as to provide a stable, prosperous environment for hundreds of employees. After fifty successful years, you'd think that our future success would be assured. As we're all acutely aware, this isn't exactly the case. There is very little autonomy in our world anymore. Information innovation moves at such lightning speed that a wide array of partnerships is necessary for all media companies in our economy to grow. However, our past does give us a head start into the future. Optimism is ingrained in our company and its employees. So is social responsibility. When our goal is to serve children, altruism and doing the right thing become necessities.

We know technology will broaden how our books are viewed and used in the coming decades. Leveraging my father's vision of our company, we will continue to meet the needs and tastes of our readership. I'm happy to say that Lerner Publishing Group is in the business of making good books for the long haul in whatever format our readers want. We'll see you in another fifty years!

—Adam Lerner
President, Lerner Publishing Group

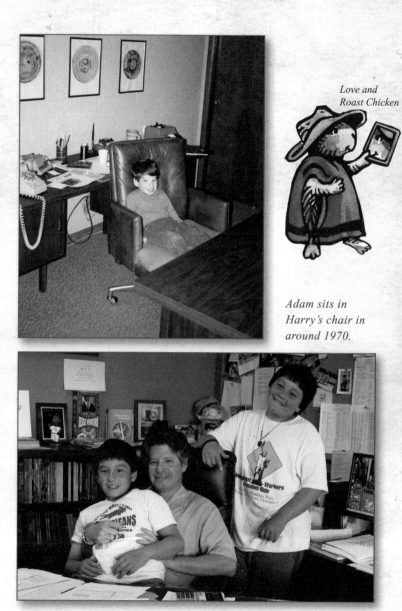

Love and Roast Chicken

Adam sits in Harry's chair in around 1970.

Now head of Lerner Publishing Group, Adam holds Leo, with Ariel standing, in 2008.

EVERY MEMOIR I'VE EVER READ listed countless friends and coworkers who affected the writer's life and the company's success, and if I didn't list these people, they'd be throwing darts at me.

Without question, longtime coworker Gary Hansen is the most knowledgeable book production person you will ever meet. He's president of Interface Graphics, our graphic arts division, and of Muscle Bound Bindery (MBB). Our creative director, Zach Marell, and before him Jim Simondet are the reasons our books look so beautiful. We sell lots of books, day in and day out, chiefly because of vice president David Wexler and director Joni Sussman. They have taken our company to a new level in both sales and marketing.

On the editorial side, we have the best and most dedicated workers any publishing house can boast. In twenty-five years, Vicki Liestman has guided books to many awards. These days she works closely with Mary Rodgers, editor in chief, and the editorial directors—Domenica Di Piazza, Kitty Creswell, Carol Hinz, Carol Burrell, and Andrew Karre—to plan our publishing program. To Vicki, 2012 is tomorrow, and 2020 is next week! I must also mention Sylvia Johnson, who edited and authored countless books for us. She is a great science writer and was difficult to replace after her retirement.

On the promotion and sales side, we have Kathleen Clarke, Brad Richason, Lois Wallentine, Terri Reden, and Maria Kjoller. Their efforts have enabled us to place our books in every nook and cranny in the country—and beyond! Our business office and distribution center is smoothly run because of our chief financial officer Margaret Wunderlich and comptroller Tracy Kill and our warehouse manager Ken Rued.

Our former in-house editor Margaret Goldstein was reenlisted to review and comment on this story, and her suggestions were most helpful. No one, of course, would have seen this at all if not for my assistant Lynn Burow, who can decipher my messy handwriting. Along the way, I have sought the advice and judgment of my wife, Sandy. Any mistakes or omissions are entirely her fault. (Just kidding.)

Finally, and once more, I must thank Mary Rodgers. It was she who encouraged me to begin this project and pushed, prodded, and even coerced until it reached its conclusion.

Guess What Is Growing Inside This Egg

IMAGINE YOU'RE GENGHIS KHAN, with your warrior horsemen sweeping through the steppes of eastern Europe. Your opponents are weak and frightened, and you're well organized to take them on. You're big and strong. Nothing can stop you. You can do it!

Or imagine you're David fighting Goliath. You're small, frightened, and fighting a bigger foe. But you're agile, you aim well. You can do it!

Most entrepreneurs won't admit it, but such fantasies are common in business. Ross Perot admired the warrior Attila the Hun and bought copies of the *Leadership Secrets of Attila the Hun* to give away. Did he imagine he was Attila?

Ted Turner says that in the early days of CNN, he thought of the company as Finland in 1939. Finland, a small country with a small population, was being invaded by Russia. Russia (the major networks) had superior forces, yet brave Finland (CNN) repelled their initial attacks. This was Ted Turner's fantasy.

Here is mine: Our duchy is stuck in the middle of Europe someplace. The time is the late Middle Ages. Our duchy is quite peaceful, while the bigger countries—England, France, Spain, and Germany—are always at one another's throats. But we go our way, almost not noticing them. We have our own resources in every respect. Our citizens are treated well. We're successful and admired by all. They, the bigger countries, leave us alone, and we leave them alone.

This has always been my fantasy about Lerner Publishing Group. We are self-contained. We purchase our own paper, do our own pre-press work, own our own bindery, and do our own selling and marketing. We treat our people well. We're the independent duchy.

That was then, this is now. Perhaps we've outgrown my fantasy concept. We've opened offices in New York and London. We have alliances with companies in Japan, China, Korea, and Australia. Canada and Mexico are our biggest foreign markets. But I hope we have not lost the coziness of our independence.

I am no longer as intensely focused on the business as I used to be. I spend more time in my workshop, with grandchildren, on the tennis court, supervising investments, and trying to keep up with the

changing technologies in publishing. I used to work six days a week—now I work only five. So I haven't slowed down much.

Here I am holding up a plaque the employees gave me when the company celebrated its thirtieth anniversary in 1989.

" I've always equated Lerner Publications with a deli in a gentrified neighborhood. You have the cantankerous father, who outlasted his adversaries by never short-changing his customers; and the wise, older son, grounded in the present but respectful of the past. Nearby, there might be larger franchises churning out volume. But the exotics behind the counter indisputably make a better sandwich. **"**

from Lerner author KEITH ELLIOT GREENBERG

" The clearest window into seeing one's own homeland often comes through the eyes of a foreigner. The Mexican way of conducting business (and many of its major problems) dawned on me after Adam and I had had an arduous meeting with a big distributor. Adam turned to me and said, "How come they can't produce a simple 'yes or no'?" Sharing my knowledge and care for the Spanish-language book market has been one of the major perks of working with Lerner. **"**

from consultant for ediciones Lerner
JUANA INÉS DEHESA CHRISTLIEB

Happy Birthday, Mallory!

A LIFELONG FRIENDSHIP

We have been doing business with Japanese children's book publishers since the 1970s. We have both bought projects from them, as well as sold some of our projects into the Japanese market. My friendships with these publishers have grown over the years. When I was still going to international fairs, I would make a point of having dinner with these friends, particularly Mr. Hidekazu Sato, a gentleman of the highest order. He usually brought with him Yurika Yokota Yoshida, who acted as translator.

Mr. Sato doesn't go to international fairs anymore either. But in 2004, Sandy and I traveled to Japan. Sato-san brought us together with many Japanese publishers. He even took us to a Japanese spa! I will always value his friendship.

While in Japan in 2004, Sandy and I enjoyed our time at a spa with Mr. Sato (left) *and Yurika.*

66 To Harry Lerner—who has pursued the difficult job of publishing books with love and pride, while running a company successfully for fifty years, and now is giving it to the next generation—I send my deepest respect and friendship. 99

from HIDEKAZU SATO,
Koguma Publishing Co., Ltd., Tokyo, Japan

66 Lerner is one of the pioneer publishers that built up friendships through publishing. Since Harry published the Lerner Natural Science Books, originally published by Akane Shobo in the 1970s, and awarded the Sharon Lerner Scholarship to Japanese editor Kayoko Yoneda in the 1980s, these friendships have become concrete year after year. No doubt they will continue forever. 99

from YURIKA YOKOTA YOSHIDA,
Japan Foreign-Rights Centre

Lots of Latkes

I DON'T KNOW ALL THE DETAILS of how my parents got to the United States, but what I do know is interesting. And I'm awed when I think about it. I can't imagine my mother as a sixteen-year-old girl and her twenty-one-year-old brother leaving their large family in Bessarabia, Russia, in 1912. They came without money, not knowing the language or any Americans.

They wound up in Aitkin in northern Minnesota, where my Uncle Mendel worked on the railroad. Not too many Jewish immigrants worked on the railroad, but Mendel was a tough guy and a pretty good mechanic. At least I know he was handy and always repairing things.

Almost upon arrival, my mother, Lena, got sick with typhoid fever. Mendel's section foreman on the railroad was an Englishman. He took a liking to Mendel and offered to have his wife look after Lena. My mother lost her hair and was sick for a long time. "Ma" Daniels nursed her back to health.

This was the beginning of a lifetime friendship with Ma and Pa Daniels. They later adopted a boy with special needs named Wilber and had no other children. Wilber often came down to Minneapolis to visit. For years and years, my mother sent the Danielses gifts, clothing, and money. In the 1960s, my mother, my wife, and I went to visit them. We were appalled at their living conditions. They still had the shack of earlier days, with no running water and an outhouse. Eventually, they moved to a nursing home. Ma Daniels's obituary mentioned my mother as her surviving daughter.

After my mother recovered from typhoid fever, it was time to move on. She and her brother left Aitkin. They moved to Rhame, a very small town in Bowman County in western North Dakota. I'll bet you can't find it on a map.

Eventually, my mother traded a cow for a cream station. That's where the farmers would deposit their milk for sale to railcars that came by. I'm not sure what my uncle did. They did have a homestead, but I don't think he ever farmed.

My mother was probably less than five feet two, medium build, unlike many of her women friends who were quite meaty. Early pictures of her show a very pretty girl, and she stayed quite attractive through her entire life. She lived to be 101 years old. At least this is what we, the family, determined. My secretary Gladys, however, did a little research and claimed she was 103 years old when she passed away.

My mother was always sensitive about her age. She would never admit how old she was. I once asked her about this when she was in her nineties. She replied that the ladies she played cards with were in their sixties and seventies, and if she revealed her true age, they would think she was senile like many others in her senior residence.

Believe it or not, this is a photo of a pogrom in Kishinev in 1903.
My father is at the far right in the first row.

My dad's story is different and equally interesting. He was the old-est of six children, born in Kishinev, in czarist Russia. You history buffs will know about the pogroms of Kishinev. What happened to my dad and his family during that period is another story and another book.

As a youth, my dad was active as a Menshevik, or Socialist. After the failed 1905 revolution, the police were rounding up troublemak-ers. The story goes that they came looking for my dad at his home one night. They left a message that he was to report to the police station the next day. That evening he said good-bye to his family and left.

He made his way through Europe and eventually found himself

in Liverpool, England. It took him six months to earn enough money for steerage to Ellis Island, where he applied for land under the Homestead Act.

While waiting for his homestead papers to come through, he traveled to Minneapolis and worked at the West Hotel. He didn't live here long. His papers came—he was assigned fifty acres near Ludlow, South Dakota. This was 1909, and my dad was twenty-one.

Ludlow is in northwestern South Dakota, close to Montana and Rhame, North Dakota. Small Jewish communities were in many parts of the Dakotas. This is where my parents met and married. My sister, Miriam, was born in Rhame in 1919.

To me, my dad always resembled the movie actor Edward G. Robinson. He had the same round face, was not tall—about five feet six—and had an apple-shaped belly.

This photo was taken in around 1947. Doesn't my dad remind you of Edward G. Robinson? That's me next to him. My brother David is at the far left. My cousin Lillian is in the middle.

Eventually, my parents moved to Minneapolis and had three more children. Me? I'm the youngest. Maybe a mistake. I'm ten years younger than my next brother.

My mother and father had a small grocery store on Nicollet Island, one of those ma and pa stores where you worked twenty-five hours a day, seven days a week. It was called Morris Island Grocery, named for my father, Morris.

The parcel of land sat inside a split of the Mississippi River. A store had long been at that location—at least I saw printed cards that said "since 1888." The address was 7 East Hennepin. But this address no longer exists. Urban renewal developed the entire street in the 1950s, and the location is now a wide sidewalk.

My parents became tenants in about 1921. The store, perhaps less than one thousand square feet, was owned by the Johnson brothers. The three brothers ran the successful Island Cycle Shop next door. They sold bicycles, repaired bikes, and distributed parts.

Our family knew the Johnson brothers well. They were good landlords and decent people, except for Art Johnson's wife, who often made anti-Semitic comments. Her nasty words made a lasting impression on me as a ten-year-old.

Art was the boss and made the business decisions. His brother Ed ran the retail side of the business, and brother George ran the repair shop. Art was the smartest, but George was the most interesting. George was blind, yet he could repair any bike. Human-interest stories about George regularly appeared in the local newspaper.

Our grocery store was open seven days a week. My father, who never drove a car, took the bus downtown every day at about

Here's my dad posing in our grocery store in the 1920s. We still have the ice-cream table and chairs somewhere in our offices.

eight in the morning. Dad kept the store open until at least eight at night and Saturdays until ten at night. The store had a small, cast-iron furnace that kept us warm in winter. We'd fill it with coal, wood, and crumbled cardboard boxes.

When Prohibition ended in 1933, my parents managed to get a liquor license. Only a few grocery stores could get liquor licenses in those days. In fact, there were only two liquor-grocery stores in all Minneapolis. The most popular beverage, other than beer, was muscatel, a wine with 20 percent alcohol content. The customers called it "mustn't tell." No one drinks it today.

My mother stands in front of Morris Island Grocery and Liquor Store in the 1940s.

Because of the strict guidelines as to when liquor could be sold, the liquor area had to be cordoned off. Our store had a metal fence surrounding the liquor shelves. The church people of Minneapolis made sure that liquor would not be easy to acquire.

My parents were never financially rewarded for their long hours and hard work. My father, a loving man, wasn't cut out for business. My mother always said he should have been a teacher or professor. Sometimes he would sit in the back of the store and ignore customers in the front. When he passed away from a coronary on February 13, 1948, at the age of sixty, the store was in debt. He owed money to the grocery jobbers and liquor wholesalers.

My brother Dave, who had moved to California, came back. His skill and hard work brought the business around. He paid off all the creditors.

We lived on Minneapolis's north side, considered the Jewish ghetto. Over the years, people have created books and videos about this unique neighborhood, with its own shops, bakeries, butchers, and theater.

The first rite of passage for boys on the north side was not the bar mitzvah. It was selling souvenir football pins at Memorial Stadium during University of Minnesota Gopher football games. Most neighborhood kids, from about the age of fourteen on, would buy buttons of different sizes and styles, maroon and gold ribbons, and pin backs. We assembled the pins and mounted them for sale on cloth-covered wooden frames. We did this for every Saturday home game. This was a selling experience none of us forgot.

My first business success was selling football pins before University of Minnesota games.

Here I am with my mother (second from left) *and siblings, Aaron* (far left), *Miriam* (center), *and David* (next to me). *This photo was taken in the mid-1990s.*

Here is what became of my siblings. My sister, Miriam, graduated from the University of Minnesota, married a psychology professor, moved to Bloomsburg, Pennsylvania, and had four children. Her husband, Marty Satz, died in 2005. Miriam had a massive heart attack in 2007 and died in 2008 at the age of eighty-nine. My eldest brother, Aaron, was a researcher and scientist, well known for his discovery of melatonin. He earned his MD and PhD degrees from the University of Minnesota in 1945. In 1955 he joined the faculty at Yale—the second-youngest full professor in the history of the university at that time. He was also the first head of the Dermatology Department at Yale Medical School (1958–1985), and he was the only dermatologist elected to the National Academy of Sciences. He passed away in 2007 at the age of eighty-six. Dave, who took over my parents' store, died in 1999 at the age of seventy-seven. His son Matt now runs the store in a different location.

I WAS A RESTLESS KID—TERRIBLE IN SCHOOL, friendly out of school, and always looking for something to do. I was active in Habonim, a Labor Zionist organization whose goal was to reclaim the Holy Land as a socialist paradise. Zionist summer camps and conferences were a highlight of my youth. This experience eventually led me to spend time in Israel in 1953–1954.

But remember the draft, when every young man was expected to serve two years in the army? It was two years if you were drafted and four if you enlisted. Guess my choice? I was drafted in my senior year at the University of Minnesota.

Fort Leonard Wood in Missouri was considered the worst place for basic training, and in my opinion, it was. The cadre had just returned from Korea, and our training was unbelievably tough for a 120-pound kid. But I felt strong and energetic.

Herman Wouk, in his book *The Caine Mutiny*, once described the navy as "designed by geniuses for execution by idiots." That description could also apply to the army. The first thing the army did, almost upon our arrival, was give everyone a written test. After the first test,

That's me in the circle. I'm carrying my U.S. Army M1 rifle. And opposite is one of my manual typewriters—an Underwood.

I was called back for further testing.

I'll never forget being rounded up with other draftees for further testing. Who were these other inductees? They were mostly from the South and were being tested for reading, as most could hardly read or write. What was I doing in this group? It turned out I was being tested as a linguist. I knew some Hebrew and had studied a little Arabic and German. They classified me as a linguist, a skill I didn't know I had.

After basic training, most of the GIs were sent to tank school or artillery training. They gave me orders to report to Fort Dix, New Jersey, where I was immediately assigned to the infantry, because they had no opening for a linguist.

With my flat feet, the infantry wasn't my first choice, or even my last. Fortunately, someone got me assigned to clerk-typist school. At that time, the army had only manual typewriters. Remember them? (By the way, I still have several of them.)

I finished clerk-typist school, and the army still didn't know what to do with a linguist. So they assigned me to shovel coal to keep the barracks warm in the cold winter of 1954. I did this job for three weeks, and for three months afterward, I coughed and sneezed up coal dust. My handkerchiefs were black. Remember handkerchiefs?

After shoveling coal, they put me on a troop ship along with a couple thousand others. It took us thirteen days to get to Bremerhaven, Germany. From Bremerhaven, a train ride took us to Ludwigshofen for further assignment.

> ❝ THEY CLASSIFIED ME AS A LINGUIST,
> A SKILL I DIDN'T KNOW I HAD. ❞

The loudspeaker bellowed out names, and trucks were loaded up. I didn't hear my name. I wasn't being called. Only a few of us were left when the speaker shouted out Lerner and Levy. A master sergeant was waiting for us in a staff car, a Ford sedan, not the standard

Jeep. I looked at my partner. Who was this guy Levy? He was tall and skinny—a chain smoker who had studied accounting at Brooklyn College.

The sergeant took us to Coleman Barracks, situated between Mannheim and Heidelberg. Thus began an amazing adventure that led to my publishing career and changed my life forever.

THE CAPTAIN WAS AN SOB

Captain Harold V. Echols was a tall, handsome Texan, with a mean streak as long as his trousers. This SOB was my commanding officer. He was a bigot of the first order. He would demote blacks for the slightest infraction. He made derogatory comments about Hispanics and was anti-Semitic. His wife often appeared at the snack shop with black-and-blue marks on her. One time I reported him to the adjutant general in Frankfurt because he wouldn't give me time off for Yom Kippur. I'm convinced I never made it past private first class (PFC) because of him.

THE ORDINANCE PROCUREMENT CORPS (OPC) was an unusual out-
fit. It was housed in a large building at Coleman Barracks. The unit
had about 50 officers, 150 mostly German civilians, and 12 EMs like
myself. *EM* stood for "enlisted men"—those who had been drafted.
Those who had signed up for four years were regular army (RA). Like
me, most of the EMs had had some college.

This was the time of the Cold War, and our enemy was the Soviet
Union. When I first arrived in Germany, we were occupation forces,
but in May 1955, our occupation ended and West Germany joined
NATO. A month later, the other side organized the Warsaw Pact, com-
prising all the Communist countries of Eastern Europe.

Even though our troops had frequent maneuvers and were getting
ready to fight the Soviets, life was easy at the OPC. If war broke out,
our unit was instructed to withdraw to Paris and regroup.

At the OPC I was a clerk-typist. But since I couldn't type well,
I spent most of my time proofreading technical specifications on
blasting caps to be manufactured in Turkey. Our hours were regular
office hours.

This Volkswagen dates from the mid-1950s. These cars were all over the place when I was stationed in Germany.

After five, most of the GIs would wander about the small towns near Coleman Barracks, spending most of their time and money at *gasthauses*, or taverns. But you could do that only so much. At least for me, enough was enough of gasthauses. I had to find other things to do.

At this time, Germany was rapidly rebuilding from the devastation of World War II. Its economy was improving. Many cities, such as Frankfurt and Mannheim, were still bombed out. Heidelberg, a university town, had been left unharmed.

Volkswagens were very popular in Germany then and were starting to make their way to the United States. "Wouldn't it be nice to have a Volkswagen franchise in Minneapolis?" I thought. I wrote to Volkswagen headquarters in Wolfsburg, asking for an appointment with the president. (Remember writing letters?) The company wrote back, asking about my experience in the auto industry. When I replied that I had extensive experience in the grocery industry and was willing to learn the auto industry, VW in essence said forget it.

Undeterred, I sent a telegram to the president of Volkswagen, Herr Heinrich Nordhoff. I said I was coming to see him, knowing there was no way they could reach me to stop me because I was already en route.

At the factory gate, I said I had an appointment with the president, and they flagged me through. I was escorted to a large reception room. The receptionist said the president would be out to see me shortly.

I looked very young for twenty-two. Most people thought I was eighteen or nineteen. I was wearing the civilian suit that I kept in the bottom of my duffle bag just for such an occasion. The brown tweed suit was wrinkled but didn't look too bad. I wore a shirt and tie.

The room was empty until an elderly gentleman, well dressed, tall, with gold cuff links and distinguished gray hair—a real Beau Brummell—came into the reception area and sat next to me on the sofa. Then Herr Nordhoff came out and quickly rushed over to the sofa. He said, "Mr. Lerner, welcome to Volkswagen," extending his hand not to me but to this other guy. I was stunned. "It's me, I'm here," I said shyly and embarrassed. Nordhoff hadn't known Mr. Lerner was just a kid. He thought the mature person sitting next to me was Mr. Lerner.

When the cast of characters was redefined, Nordhoff ushered me into his large office, and we chatted for a while. He said the only opening was in Cedar Rapids, Iowa, and he didn't think I was ready for the job. So much for this project. I started looking for something else.

When You Visit
Grandma & Grandpa

GIs WERE IMPORTING AMERICAN CARS at U.S. government expense or purchasing their own European cars. I bought a 1950 French Renault for about three hundred dollars. I drove this car all over Germany and parts of France, Luxembourg, and Denmark. It was a Renault 4CV, much smaller than a Volkswagen. It had wind-catching suicide doors. The engine was in the rear. Color: green. The loose floorboard gave me a good view of the pavement. Twice I came to an abrupt halt when the engine fell off its mountings, but fortunately I found a German mechanic who could put it back together again.

Later, I purchased a sporty Volkswagen Karmann Ghia, the most beautiful car in the world, I thought. New, it cost seventeen hundred dollars, which I borrowed from my mother and brother Dave. I drove it through Europe. After I got back to Minneapolis, I sold it for twenty-three hundred dollars.

Here is how my first book came about. My idea was to write a book for GIs in Germany that would tell them everything they needed to know about foreign cars and travel. I knew there was a need for such a book. It would be a sort of "blue book," with information on

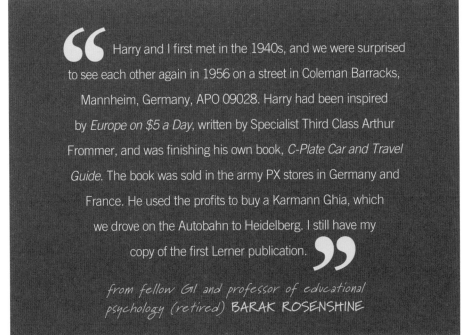

> Harry and I first met in the 1940s, and we were surprised to see each other again in 1956 on a street in Coleman Barracks, Mannheim, Germany, APO 09028. Harry had been inspired by *Europe on $5 a Day*, written by Specialist Third Class Arthur Frommer, and was finishing his own book, *C-Plate Car and Travel Guide*. The book was sold in the army PX stores in Germany and France. He used the profits to buy a Karmann Ghia, which we drove on the Autobahn to Heidelberg. I still have my copy of the first Lerner publication.
>
> *from fellow GI and professor of educational psychology (retired)* BARAK ROSENSHINE

car prices, as well as information on insurance, international driver's licenses, and other topics.

At that time, all U.S. personnel, both military and civilian, had license plates with a *C* before the number. These plates enabled us to purchase gas for fourteen cents a gallon at post exchange (PX) gas stations. That gave me my book's title, *C-Plate Car and Travel Guide*.

The German librarian at our base library was helpful. I wrote to dozens of travel bureaus and auto manufacturers gathering information. Mail was coming from all over for Private First Class Harry Lerner. My manuscript was taking shape.

Here I am in 1955 in my green 1950 French Renault.

I knew the only place to sell this book was through the *Stars and Stripes* newsstands that were ubiquitous at army bases. I took a day off and drove up to Darmstadt, the headquarters and distribution center for *Stars and Stripes*. I located the person who made the purchasing decisions, Jack Label, and he liked my idea. He said he'd take ten thousand copies at a discount of 40 percent off the retail price. We determined that sixty-five cents would be a good selling price. Surely, I could get the book printed for less than the thirty-nine cents per copy I was to receive.

We struck a deal. I was to get the book printed and delivered to the *S&S* warehouse in Darmstadt. Oh, one other thing. Label said I would need to give him a letter from my commanding officer that said I wrote it on my own time, not during working hours. I gulped as I left his office.

SIGN HERE

One of my duties in the army was to take documents to either Captain Echols or Captain Maurice Schneider for signature. Here was my chance to get the letter Jack Label said I needed. I was pretty sure Echols wouldn't sign such a document. But Schneider wasn't so bad. I typed a letter saying that Private First Class Harry Lerner had written *C-Plate Car and Travel Guide* on his own time, after duty hours, and slipped it in between other documents that Captain Schneider was to sign. With a pounding heart, I gave him the stack of papers.

As he was penning his signature, he yelled out, "What's this, Lerner?" I said, "Oh, it's nothing. Just a routine request." He continued signing. Nothing was ever said about this again. The fact was I actually did write the book on my own time.

I looked around for a printer and wound up at the local Socialist newspaper, the *Allgemeine Zeitung* in Mannheim. There I met the publisher, Herr Benz, and his assistant, Fraulein Wagner. Herr Benz was a nice man, who liked his beer and wienerschnitzel. Benz gave me a

EXCERPT FROM *C-PLATE CAR AND TRAVEL GUIDE*

European driving habits are different from ours. First off, they're unaccustomed to traffic regulations, they have so few, and speed limits are practically nonexistent. One habit typically German is when the driver in front of you decides to make a right turn, he'll first swing left, all indication pointing to a left turn, then swing his vehicle right into the next road. Why is it that those continental manners disappear immediately when a German seats himself behind the wheel? Perhaps the English are the most sensible of the Europeans, even if their traffic does flow to the left. To the English, an auto is merely transportation, not to be used as a scare machine. Perhaps the French are the most reckless.

But that's my opinion. Some say the Italian drivers are worse, and others claim the Spanish top the list. The American is still the best driver. Mox nix [a GI's phonetic spelling of the German words *macht nichts* (doesn't matter)] what anyone else says.

quote, which I thought was reasonable, and we shook hands on the deal. All I had to do was finish the manuscript, get it legibly typed, and bring it in.

But I was still a terrible typist and didn't have my own typewriter. Here's what I did. I got our unit's supply sergeant to lend me an old manual typewriter for a week. Then I searched out typing schools in Mannheim. There were many schools. Most of the students were women. But each one wanted too many deutschmarks for typing my manuscript.

I thought that by hanging around the schools at six o'clock, when they usually let out, perhaps I could find a willing student who would type the manuscript on her own time using my borrowed typewriter.

I lucked out on my first try. Inga was about eighteen. She was perfect—a capable typist, likable, and living at home with her parents. She said she'd have the job done in a week.

The next week, I went to pick it up. Her mother said she had worked very late every night typing it, as English was a challenge for her. She didn't know what to charge, so I offered forty

This picture of me was taken outside our barracks. I developed the picture myself, which is why it's so grainy.

deutschmarks, which was about ten dollars at the time. The mother said that was too much and accepted only after my determined insistence. I thought the price was a bargain, and both mother and daughter thought it was too much. Wish that I could find more like them.

When I had completed the manuscript, I brought it into the office of the Mannheimer *Allgemeine Zeitung*. After exchanging a few pleasantries, in halting German on my part, Herr Benz said he had some bad news. In checking our agreement with his attorney, he said he couldn't go through with producing the book because U.S. soldiers stationed in Germany could not be held liable for payment. "But," I said, "we had a deal. We shook hands!"

Fraulein Wagner saw how upset I was and came over to calm me down. I invited her out to dinner to discuss the situation. She was very efficient in her job as assistant to Herr Benz. She spoke some English. After many meetings and dinners, she convinced her boss to show good faith; she had confidence I'd take care of the printing bill after payment from *Stars and Stripes*. Thank you, Fraulein Wagner!

After turning in the manuscript, I left for a vacation, leaving the proofing job to my two best army friends, John Sloan and Marty Levy. They read it, okayed it, and had it printed. Off to Darmstadt it went.

It turned out, the proofing job had been lousy. But lots of errors didn't stop the book from selling. My first check from *Stars and Stripes* was for five hundred dollars, which I proudly exhibited to my unit. Considering that army pay was about seventy-five dollars a month in 1956, this was a windfall. Eventually, I even prepaid the printing bill before it was due because the book sold so well. "When I get out of the army," I said to myself, "publishing is definitely something to look into."

I WAS RELEASED FROM THE ARMY in the fall of 1956 and had three quarters to complete to graduate from the University of Minnesota. My major was international relations. Before my army service, my thinking was to become a diplomat, working for the foreign service. This major was the logical step in that direction.

Serving overseas in the army changed my mind. A number of Americans in foreign service had worked at the OPC, and I quickly learned that their life wasn't for me. Advancement in the State Department was slow and grinding. Promotions were based on seniority, usually not on aptitude and ability. But I still wanted to get a BA without backtracking, so I continued in the international relations major.

Don Goldfus was a very close friend going back to junior high. He had recently been discharged from the air force and was looking for something to do. Don was very smart. I knew this from high school, where he never studied and still got good grades. (By contrast, I studied a lot and hardly got passing grades.)

This is the Lumber Exchange Building where Sporting Goods Journal (above left) *was printed and where I had an office.*

After military service, Don had attended the University of Minnesota briefly and then decided that was enough. By then, I knew I wanted to work in publishing. I suggested to Don that we start a magazine about the sporting equipment business. I had seen *Wallpaper Digest* and *Lumberyard Journal* grow, and I figured that trade industry magazines were the coming thing. Although most would find reading these publications a cure for insomnia, I could see they were thriving. Someone was staying awake.

Without any experience and only a little savings, we enticed the printer in the Lumber Exchange Building in downtown Minneapolis to print our magazine, *Sporting Goods Journal*. Don and a fellow named Bob Hubbard wrote most of the articles, and Don and I tried to sell advertising space. I paid Don twenty-five dollars a week from my savings account.

It was a good magazine, but we were not successful and printed only four issues. We sold the magazine to another entrepreneur, who, after a small down payment, defaulted on the balance.

Don wanted to get married and had to find other work. He took a job with Harmon Glass, a windshield glass replacement and repair shop. In a few short years, he advanced from advertising manager to vice president. Harmon Glass eventually became Apogee Enterprises, Inc., one of the largest corporations in Minnesota. Don was its president and CEO. He made a lot of money. He and his wife, Terri, retired to Las Vegas and have a gorgeous home. We still keep in touch with visits and e-mail.

> **"** In late 1958, I received a phone call from my high school buddy, Harry Lerner. He asked if I would like to join him in a new venture, publishing a trade magazine. Not having a job—and with the lure of a $25 per week paycheck—I agreed. Thus was born the short-lived *Sporting Goods Journal*, the self-professed leader in Midwest sporting goods journalism and the predecessor of the Lerner Publishing empire. **"**
>
> *from* DON GOLDFUS

MARGIE RUSH WAS A STUDENT at the University of Minnesota when she met my brother Aaron. She was outgoing and very popular. Her majors were English and theater arts, and she often acted in college plays. Aaron and Margie were married in 1945, shortly after Aaron received his combination MD and PhD degrees. (It was wartime, and the Army Specialized Training Program was awarding dual degrees to accelerate gifted students for the war effort.)

When Aaron was stationed in Staten Island, examining incoming refugees, Margie decided to apply to medical school. She had no trouble gaining admittance, as she was brilliant. Once, when I accused her of never receiving a grade less than A, she corrected me, saying she'd once received a B+ in an advanced chemistry class at Johns Hopkins. If she got a B+, I'd like to meet the genius who got an A.

After Aaron's military service, he accepted a position at the University of Michigan Medical School in Ann Arbor. Both Margie and Aaron worked and taught at the medical school and the university hospital while raising a family of four boys. This is where Margie

At top are the covers for three of our first medical books. Below those is marketing material.

had the idea of writing children's books about medical topics, using humor and verse and covering basic information.

Her first manuscripts were *Michael Gets the Measles* and *Peter Gets the Chickenpox*, which the big publishing houses rejected. She also wanted to write about the other major childhood diseases of the time. But no publisher was interested, so Aaron and Margie asked me to get involved. The year was 1959, and my *Sporting Goods Journal* was winding down.

Aaron was willing to invest three thousand dollars for the first four books—three about childhood diseases and a single book, *Doctors' Tools*, on the instruments doctors use. I'll jump ahead to tell you that after the initial success, we added more and more subjects to what became Medical Books for Children. We put out books on penicillin, hands, feet, hair, hearing, and the only book for children on left-handedness.

Then Margie wrote *Red Man, White Man, African Chief*, about the scientific explanation of skin color. It was very successful, as were our other titles. *Red Man* won an award from the National Conference

My sister-in-law Margie Lerner (far left) *receives an award from an officer of the National Conference of Christians and Jews for her book* Red Man, White Man, African Chief *that discusses skin pigmentation. Author Cornelia Otis Skinner looks on.*

> **❝** Sometime in the 1960s, my grandparents, Garry and Caroline Myers, founders of *Highlights for Children*, met Harry Lerner. The occasion was the awarding of a Brotherhood Award given by the National Conference of Christians and Jews. I believe Lerner Publications and *Highlights* were both receiving an award. One of the joys of meeting Harry in the 1990s was to have him recount that evening. I immediately knew Harry as a person my grandparents admired, and he admired them. They were pioneers in publishing and brotherhood. **❞**
>
> *from Boyds Mills publisher* **KENT L. BROWN JR.**

of Christians and Jews—our first and at that time most significant award. Burt Weisberg, a good friend and our company attorney, attended the awards ceremony with me. It was a black-tie event in New York, and we rented our tuxes. Johnny Carson was the host; journalist Sander Vanocur and humorist Sam Levenson presented the award.

Red Man, White Man, African Chief

IN 1960 I WAS LOOKING FOR A DATE to take to the Aquatennial parade in downtown Minneapolis. A friend, Bob Krishef, suggested I call Sharon Goldman, someone I didn't know and had never heard of.

I met Sharon in 1960. Here we are at a Minnesota Education Association meeting before we got married.

She was perfect—bright, attractive, and petite.

She was studying at the College of Education to become an art teacher. She was interested in world affairs, well read, and very industrious as she had to work at a variety of jobs to earn her tuition. She was a cashier at a local theater, worked in the kitchen at University Hospital, and worked as an assistant art teacher at University High School. Her parents' home was near campus, and she knew her way around the school well.

Daisy Tudebaker—*a 1954 yellow station wagon*—*was our second car.*

A little over a year later, we were married. Sharon continued to teach for a couple of years after we got married. We had a small apartment in southeast Minneapolis and one car, a 1955 Oldsmobile, a gift from Uncle Mendel. We alternated its use. One day I'd take the bus to my office in the Lumber Exchange Building, and she'd take the car to her job in White Bear Lake. The next day I drove the car to work, and she'd get a ride with another teacher who lived nearby. The other teacher would also drive when I needed the car to visit printers to make press checks. Eventually, I bought a used yellow 1954 Studebaker station wagon, which Sharon dubbed *Daisy Tudebaker*.

Robins: Songbirds of Spring

> " I remember calling on Harry when he opened his small office in the Lumber Exchange Building in downtown Minneapolis. I insured a very modest amount of inventory [for him], including a typewriter that he rented for $10 (such a deal!). "
>
> *from Lerner friend* **ARNIE RIBNICK**

The next five years, before we had children, was a time of growth for our business. Sharon left teaching and worked with me to expand our publishing company. She was the art director and the perfect brainstormer.

Sharon was not only artistic, she was creative. She made jewelry (above) *and painted. We loved brainstorming new ideas.*

Eventually, I bought a Yamaha street bike that Sharon and I took out for spins on the weekends.

We felt free. Although we watched our expenses, we traveled everywhere, mostly for business and book fairs. We went to movies whenever we felt like it. We ate out a lot. We were the perfect young couple. We shared thoughts, habits, and a common goal of making our publishing house a success. After a couple of years, we moved to Plymouth, a suburb of Minneapolis, to a small house about fifteen miles from downtown.

OUR KIDS

As you all know, having children changes your life forever.

After two miscarriages, Adam was born in 1966, followed by

another miscarriage. Then Mia came along in 1969. Danny

arrived in 1971, and in 1978 Leah was born.

This family photo was taken in 1980. The dog's name was Esau.

Sail Away, Little Boat

I THINK IT WAS AROUND 1961 that Sharon and I attended a play at Scott Hall at the University of Minnesota. It was a boring play, and during intermission, I wandered the halls of the building. There it was—a big poster hanging on the wall above the piano. This illustrated poster showed everything there was to know about the piano—its history and development, and types of pianos—all beautifully designed. I thought, what a nice book this would make. And why stop at the piano? What about the other instruments?

But an idea is not enough. I needed someone who knew music, had teaching experience, could write, and would do the work for a low price, no more than two hundred dollars a book. I interviewed quite a few people but had no takers. Then someone suggested I talk to an instructor at the University of Minnesota who was there for only the summer session. He was the talented Robert Surplus. He could not only play every instrument, he could also write well. He knew everything there was to know about every instrument and its history, as well as conducting, musical notation, music theory, and so on.

Sharon and I with Bob Surplus and Jean Craig at the National Music Association Conference

We planned a series of twelve books called Musical Books for Young People to come out between 1962 and 1963. Six books would be about instruments (the cover of *Keyboard Instruments* is to the left), and the other six would cover other aspects of music, such as folk music, musical organizations, and even famous music halls. (Sharon wrote this last book, called *Places of Musical Fame.*)

But Bob Surplus had personal problems, so it was a tough summer. We had him over for dinner several times a week, using the time to coax him to continue writing. He started to wither after six books, so we enlisted his girlfriend, Jean Craig, who was teaching at Oberlin College in Ohio, to help out.

Of course, the illustrator of choice was George Overlie. George was originally from Austin, Minnesota. He had attended the Phoenix School of Design in New York City. He was also one of the brave soldiers lucky enough to have survived the 1944 Normandy landing.

Here's how I met George. One day in the summer of 1959, I happened to be in the old 512 Nicollet Building visiting our family attorney, Frank Weisberg. I spotted a sign posted on the next door that read "George Overlie, Artist." He wasn't in, so I slipped my card under his door with a note saying I wanted to talk to him. This was the beginning of a very long and rewarding relationship. In my opinion, George is the most varied and talented artist our firm ever had. He can sketch in pencil and pen and ink. Watercolor is his favorite. He is also terrific with oils and acrylics. In those days,  we didn't have a way to typeset musical notes, so for the music books, George used a stick-on material and set every note by hand.

I started to presell the series in 1962 before it was published, and most of the jobbers (wholesalers) took them. At the American Library Association (ALA) convention, I met Dave Busse, vice president of

George Overlie and I have been friends for decades. Here we are in my office in 2008. Above is George in his younger days.

> **"** I met Harry Lerner when he was a very young man. At that time, children's books were not considered very important in the total publishing scheme. Most of the major houses had a children's book department tucked away somewhere. Then along comes Harry. He may have been one of the first to examine children's book publishing from a business point of view. He forged ground by deciding to concentrate on informational books. I used to run into Harry at industry events. While everyone else felt they were on a literary crusade, Harry kept his work in perspective. He would cause many of the grandes dames of the time to purse a lip or raise an eyebrow. I was still new to the children's books scene and somewhat shy. I didn't have the courage to shout, "Right on, Harry!" in the middle of a tea party or CBC board meeting—but in looking back, I wish I had. **"**
>
> *from fellow publisher and*
> *founder of Millbrook Press* **JEAN REYNOLDS**

Children's Press. He ordered five hundred sets of twelve—but I had only six books completed. My skills of stalling were honed here. Eventually, we produced all twelve books, and they sold well. But the name of our company had to be changed from Medical Books for Children to Lerner Publications.

IN THE EARLY 1960s, I received an unsolicited manuscript about an old man named Mr. Bumba, who was kind to kids in his neighborhood. At that time, we didn't get a lot of submissions, and I read every one we got. The story was well done and cute. It had short, choppy sentences, which I liked. I thought it had a lot of appeal for children.

The book was divided into six chapters. Since each chapter stood as a separate story, why not produce six individual books? The first one was *Mr. Bumba's New House.* The author was Pearl Augusta Harwood, a former schoolteacher living in San Diego. She was wonderful to work with. Eventually, she wrote more than twenty books for us—all illustrated by George Overlie. I didn't want anyone to think we were a one-artist publisher. So I gave George at least four other names, including Joseph Folger, Mark Springer, and Rov Andre.

George and I talked a lot about what Mr. Bumba should look like. I wanted a kind, gentle face, recognizable to

Our Friend
M R.
BUMBA

everyone. Three figures came to mind: Pappy Yokum, Pope John XXIII, and Mr. Magoo. That was the combination that worked. George made a clay model of the face so he could turn it in any direction and still keep the right look. I still have that clay figure sitting on my desk.

There was a lot of talk about school integration in the 1960s. In 1957 nine black children had integrated Central High School in Little Rock, Arkansas. President Lyndon Johnson had his War on Poverty in full swing. Busing schoolchildren was just getting started. In keeping with these efforts, I wanted to show racial diversity in Mr. Bumba's neighborhood. I was pleased that George and Pearl agreed. This brings me to something I've always liked about publishing—I can do anything I want.

I still have George's little clay sculpture (left) *of Mr. Bumba in my office. On the previous page is a poster we did of the character after we launched the series with* Mr. Bumba's New Home (below).

Every day Bill and Jane helped Mr. Bumba paint.

Soon the house was white all over, with green trimming.

Soon the kitchen was yellow.

Soon the living room was green.

Soon the bedroom was blue.

Soon the bathroom was pink and white.

This interior spread shows Jane, the African American girl character, painting. Most children's book publishers weren't commissioning actual multicultural art, but we were!

At that time, some publishers used a Benday screen over existing art to try to make characters look black. But it didn't look natural. Instead, George drew the girl in the story as an African American. The children all looked realistic. I believe this was the first attempt to have multicultural original art in children's books.

Most of our customers liked the artwork. We did get flack from some areas of the country, however. People accused us of being Communists.

MOST READERS DO NOT PAY A LOT OF ATTENTION to typefaces—unless they are unreadable. This is one area in which I've always had an interest. It is important that the typeface is clean, with proper density and the line length not too long, certainly not longer than four inches in width. And the line spacing must be appropriate. I've always admired books published by David Godine. He prided himself on using the right type in each of his books. This guy is a genuine typophile.

Originally, our early books were set on a linotype machine with monotype heads. This was an expensive and tedious process involving lines of metal type. Then came phototype, which uses photographic paper and film. It was cleaner and much better than linotype and monotype, but stripping in corrections always added immensely to the cost—sometimes more than the original quote we'd get from the typesetter. The computer changed all that. Typesetting today is easy and inexpensive.

Most of my early books were set in Times Roman or Century Schoolbook. I didn't care much for Garamond or Patina but used them occasionally. Except for headings, I stayed away from sans-serif type.

TYPE FOR THIS BOOK

Years ago, publishers would tell you about a book's production in the colophon at the back of the book. It was sort of a biography of the typefaces, typesetters, and other production information related to that title. You don't see many colophons these days.

The main text of the book you're looking at right now was set in 10 on 17 (10/17) Times New Roman. This means the type is 10 points in size and the leading is 17 points. Times New Roman is an interesting font. Two people at the London *Times* newspaper designed it in 1931 to replace and update the old font, Times Old Roman, that the paper had used for decades. The captions are set in 9/12 Times New Roman Italic, and the chapter heads are 11/13 Courier Bold.

A sans-serif typeface doesn't have those little tails at the end of each letter, and the width of the line is uniform. Serif type is just the opposite.

Wouldn't it be nice to design a type that could actually make reading easier? Especially for children just learning to read? I once ran across a typeface that had this potential. It was a rarely used face called Biltmore, which combined both serif and sans-serif features.

We typeset the Mr. Bumba series, as well as other titles, in a font that came to be called Mr. Bumba Text.

Since it was so rarely used, I asked the typesetter (the Beissel Company) to change the name to Mr. Bumba Text, and the company agreed.

We published about fifty books in Mr. Bumba Text, and I advertised its unique ability to enable the eyes to glide smoothly across the page. Here is a page from a Mr. Bumba brochure we sent out in 1965.

I was tempted to write copy saying: "This reading typeface is so unique, so revolutionary, that by its very nature it will render all other learning programs obsolete. The specially designed combination type has serif and fine hairline curlicues that only your retina can detect. Clinical trials suggest this will enhance brain development. Studies have shown a 10 percent increase in reading speed and an 8 percent increase in reading comprehension." Of course, none of this is true. No trials ever took place. But I do think about it, and I do believe there are possibilities in designing typefaces to enhance reading.

How the Guinea Fowl Got Her Spots

WHY ON EARTH would anyone want to get into the bookbinding business? Didn't someone say that necessity is the mother of invention? In this case, it was necessity and also opportunity.

In 1959 we created our first brochure, advertising our first four books: *Michael Gets the Measles, Peter Gets the Chickenpox, Dear Little Mumps Child,* and *Doctors' Tools.* I bought a bunch of labels, hand typed on perforated paper by Nelson Mailing Service, a one-man operation in the Plymouth Building in downtown Minneapolis. For an extra fee, Mr. Nelson would give you an extra carbon copy for a second mailing. It was a lot of work affixing those labels in the evenings—and by myself.

Soon, orders started to trickle in. But the response was not what I had anticipated. I had thought our market was bookstores, department stores, and hospital gift shops. I had sent brochures to public libraries as an afterthought. Yet most of the orders came from public libraries, and most of the libraries wanted "library binding."

At that time, the only bindery in town was A. J. Dahl Company, run by four brothers named Mjos. They were very nice people. Bud Mjos

Schoolkids liked coming through the bindery to see how books were manufactured.

ran the office and sales, and brother Clarence was the shop foreman. The other brothers worked in the shop.

As we added titles to the Medical Books for Children series, our volume with A. J. Dahl kept increasing. I continually kept after them to give us a break on price. I even guaranteed them five hundred thousand books a year, but Bud wouldn't budge on his prices.

One day, a very interesting man came to visit me. He was tall and lanky Paul Lund. Paul owned Lund Bindery, a small hand book bindery on Chicago Avenue, and was looking for work. It was a family affair. His wife, Winnie; daughter, Paula; and sons, Jimmy and Peter, all worked there. He said our books would be easy to bind. He could do the side sewing I wanted and would give me a price break. He would charge me two bits (twenty-five cents) a book, regardless of quantity, size, or number of pages. Paul and I became fast friends.

Reader's Digest once ran a series of articles on the most unforgettable people you'll ever met. Paul was one of those. Although of limited education, he was very bright. He made it a point to read every book he bound. He drifted from print shop to print shop before setting up Lund Bindery.

As time went on, our quantities were increasing. Paul didn't have room and time to handle our books together with his other jobs. He asked us to give him space in our building solely for binding our books. We helped him buy a few pieces of equipment, and he set up a separate bindery. He had four or five people working there.

> **"** Some of the very early Lerner books, including *Dear Little Mumps Child* about the now virtually eradicated childhood disease, were among the first books I owned as a little girl. My dad, a Holocaust survivor, who was just getting into the Minneapolis printing business, had received them as gifts from up-and-coming young publisher Harry Lerner. I still have some of those books. **"**
>
> *from publisher of Kar-Ben* JONI SUSSMAN

But Paul's attendance at work was sporadic at best. He spent a lot of time in Dillon, Montana, fishing and reading. When I had to reach him, I'd call the local public library in Dillon and leave a message. Everyone at the library knew him.

One day Paul came in and said, "Harry, pay me for this equipment and the bindery is yours." That's how I became a bookbinder.

Where did we get the name Muscle Bound? In the 1960s, most libraries required books to meet binding specifications determined by the Book Manufacturing Institute. This meant reinforced end papers, side sewing, sturdy covers, and at least a ninety-point binder's board.

I needed a name that meant strength. Gibraltar Binding, Hercules Binding, Atlas Binding, and Spartan Binding were already taken by the large New York publishers. I was on the verge of using Sampson Binding. But one morning while shaving and flexing my muscles in the mirror, the name Muscle Bound occurred to me. It's the only company in the world named after my body!

My work was tiring: editing, publishing, and selling books and, at the same time, running a bindery. The help was getting ornery, and the time clock was abused. I needed a bindery foreman and fast.

I took out a classified ad in the Minneapolis paper, Sunday edition. I'll never forget what happened next. I didn't expect a call until Monday or later in the week. But that same Sunday, I was working very late in the office when the phone rang. The fellow at the other end introduced himself as Jerry Hanson. He was working night shift at a printer, on a folder machine, and wanted to change jobs.

Thanksgiving
Rules

He also worked part-time at his father-in-law's liquor store. He thought life had more to offer.

Jerry took to book manufacturing like Tiger Woods to golf. He became so proficient and so well known in the industry that people called from all over the country asking for solutions to binding problems. There is no question that the bindery's growth was due to Jerry's skill as a manager. Because of his mechanical ability, he fully understood innovations and changes in bindery equipment. We sometimes poured millions of dollars into new equipment chiefly because I had complete confidence in Jerry's judgment.

Jerry Hanson (far left), *along with the mayor and other dignitaries, was there when we broke ground to build Muscle Bound Bindery in Minneapolis in January 1983. It was twenty degrees below zero!*

Jerry and I had a perfect understanding, although never articulated. I didn't interfere with the day-to-day operation of the bindery and took part in only major decisions that involved finances, expansion of the building, new equipment, or personnel issues, like the time a union wanted to organize our workforce. Our workers finally realized they were better off with a benevolent employer, who often exceeded union benefits, than joining a dues-paying union whose organizers knew nothing about our business.

Jerry was responsible for Muscle Bound's success, turning it from a small hand bindery into a fully equipped modern book bindery, now situated in a seventy-thousand-square-foot building in North Minneapolis. In 2004 Jerry retired after thirty-six years.

Top: *Here's how the bindery looked in the mid-1980s.* Bottom: *Muscle Bound Bindery is capable of binding soft covers and hard covers. Its state-of-the-art equipment gives customers a wide choice of binding options.*

I MOVED INTO THE 133 FIRST AVENUE NORTH BUILDING in the summer of 1962. It was a cute little three-story building, with a basement as well. Each floor had about fifteen hundred square feet for a total of six thousand square feet. The previous owner was a paper wholesaler. I was able to purchase the building for $10,500, which I borrowed from my mother. She held the note, which I dutifully paid off at $125 per month, including interest.

I had one assistant, Janet, who worked part-time. When I was traveling or exhibiting at ALA, she'd put in full days at the office. One time when I returned from a trip, she told me the fire marshal had paid us a visit. After one look at the messy, box-loaded basement, he had given us a week to clean it up. Actually, I had two days' notice, since I had been out of town most of the week.

When the fire marshal returned, I accompanied him to the basement, trying to explain why I needed more time. He said, "I gave you enough time" and proceeded to write me a ticket. He was so abrupt, nasty, and confrontational that I started to ask questions: What type of

Zvuvi's Israel

*I loved this little building at 133 First Avenue North.
Too bad we outgrew it. Worse that I sold it!*

violation was I guilty of? What exact code or statute was I violating? By whose authority had he issued me a citation?

I didn't win any points with him, and a court hearing was scheduled for the next week. The fire marshal showed up with the city attorney, and I was alone before the elderly, black-robed judge one Monday morning in August 1962.

I was young and nervous and had never appeared before a judge before. Moreover, I was ready to admit to the judge that the basement was a mess—that I was guilty and only needed more time to clean it up.

The city attorney made a convincing case. He said Lerner's basement was a fire hazard. He said I had ignored the warning and, above all, questioned the fire marshal's authority. The judge stopped the city attorney immediately after hearing that I had questioned the fire marshal. He came to my defense with an argument I never even thought of, and I did not have to say a word.

The judge said, "Lerner had a perfect right to question inspectors. Today there are so many building inspectors—there is the health inspector, the elevator inspector, the electrical inspector, the insurance inspector. There are so many inspectors that Lerner had a perfect right to question the fire marshal. Case dismissed."

A Year in a Castle

THE FIRST ALA CONFERENCE Sharon and I went to was in 1963, at the Fontainebleau Hotel in Miami Beach, Florida. ALA was the biggest book show of the time. Bigger than BookExpo America today. All the publishers were there. The big ones thought they owned the show—leaving hardly any room for small upstart publishers who wanted only one booth. And applying late for space didn't help.

The only exhibit space left was up in the balcony, called the Promenade. That's where the newcomers were, and hardly anyone would walk up the stairs to see us. We were new and had no idea what our booth should look like. We had two easels showing our Medical Books for Children and some dummies of our new series, Musical Books for Children. Whenever someone did come up the stairs, huffing and puffing, each exhibitor literally tried to pull him or her into the booth.

On one side of us was the Hammond Map Company, and across from us was Sam Goody Records. For four and a half days, we really got to know one another. It became very much like a summer camp. We shared meals and stories, and the camaraderie was

A bank in Minneapolis let us display our books in its lobby. Note the name change: we had become Lerner Publications Co.

intense. Our friendship with those exhibitors—Hugh Johnson (Hammond) and Max Schaffner (Sam Goody)—lasted years. Both have since passed away.

I also met my best publishing friend and mentor, David Boehm, at this ALA. We met wandering the aisles of the exhibit hall and hit it off immediately. David was about twenty years older than I.

He had started Sterling Publishing in 1949, first publishing game and stamp books for collectors, then craft books. He wound up publishing *The Guinness Book of World Records*. He lived into his nineties, always enjoying life with each of his five wives. Two died, and he divorced three. His son, Lincoln, took over the business. He expanded it and eventually sold it to Barnes & Noble for big bucks.

On the last day of that first ALA, when the bell rang and everyone started to tear down, Sharon yelled, "Hey, where's everyone going?" I saw a small tear swelling out of the side of her left eye. This was the life we loved.

> **"** Harry and his publishing house in so many ways resemble me and mine. We can be called brother publishers, and I'm proud of that. I met him early on and helped him stay on the right track! **"**
>
> *from the late* DAVID BOEHM

Peanut Butter and Jellyfishes

MY FIRST EXPERIENCE SELLING BOOKS was through direct mail. At the time, I didn't know much about direct marketing. I only knew that some announcement had to be made to bookstores, hospital gift shops, and department stores. Public libraries, which also appeared on the lists we purchased from R. R. Bowker (which tracks businesses in the book industry), were an afterthought.

At first, I did the mailings by myself. This lasted for a few months, until eventually I had about a dozen stay-at-home moms handling them. Then I started to experiment with different approaches. I would often mail the identical piece twice to the same potential customers. I would change the colors or use colored paper. I would change prices. Then I'd keep track of the results. I'd learn which mailing pulled best and what price point sold more books. Was an offer of $29.98 better than $30? Was $49.95 better than $50? How about a $200 offer? I tested all these possibilities.

Using this kind of experimentation, I discovered that results were better with an envelope mailing. But the additional cost of the envelopes and inserts didn't seem to warrant the expense. So I settled on

*Tooth Fairy's
First Night*

*Here are some of my direct mail
pieces from the early days.*

self-mailers, bombarding schools and libraries with an assortment of offers. My goal at the time was to mail each and every school and public library in the country one piece of mail each week during the school year. I didn't quite achieve that goal, but I came close.

I thought our Medical Books for Children would make excellent waiting-room reading material for children in doctors' and dentists' offices. So I tried an experiment. I sent out a mailing to doctors and dentists. One-half of the brochures offered any four books for $10, and the other half offered the same four books for $9.95. Which offer pulled best? The $9.95 won out by a landslide. I didn't think a nickel would make a difference to medical professionals, but I guess they think like everyone else. By the way, in selling to medical professionals, the biggest bargain hunters are dentists.

> IN SELLING TO MEDICAL PROFESSIONALS, THE BIGGEST BARGAIN HUNTERS ARE DENTISTS.

A wonderful organization called the Upper Midwest Direct Mail Club started in Minneapolis in the early 1960s. It began as a small group of mailers and gradually grew to include some of the major companies in our region. I became an active member.

Members shared ideas with one another. Monthly programs addressed design concepts, brochures, mailing lists, and other topics. We hosted speakers from the post office as well as advertising executives. The group was a big success and eventually changed its name to the Direct Marketing Club.

Times change. With the increased cost of postage and mailing lists, we have, over time, redirected our efforts into real human beings, who represent us to schools and libraries. Our sales reps now number around 150. We have three distinct selling groups: trade, school classrooms, and libraries (both school and public).

I Know an Old Teacher

WE'VE ALWAYS ENJOYED PUBLISHING ART BOOKS. Sharon was an art teacher, first at University High in Minneapolis and later at Sunrise Junior High in White Bear Lake.

Most art teachers spend much of their teaching time on arts and crafts. But Sharon always thought there was more to art than that. She spent a lot of time trying to instill an appreciation of the fine arts. But the kids were not always receptive. In fact, they were quite rowdy. Even in seventh grade, many were bigger than her five foot one. You can imagine a petite teacher with mischievous kids throwing paper, crayons, and pencils around the classroom.

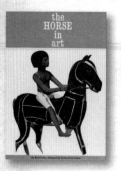

But Sharon was determined to show them something about the world of art—the masters—something they would appreciate for the rest of their lives. She thought the subject approach might work. Kids of all ages are interested in horses. So why not teach them

The first of our Fine Art Books was
The Horse in Art.

how great artists have depicted horses through the years—starting with the Lascaux Caves, covering Franz Marc's *Blue Horses*, up to current times.

This was a gem of an idea that led to our Fine Art Books for Young People (1965–1972). Sharon gathered her art cronies to brainstorm the subjects. We initially made a list of six subjects: *The Horse in Art, The Ship and the Sea in Art, Kings and Queens in Art, The Self-Portrait in Art, Farms and Farmers in Art,* and *Circuses and Fairs in Art.* We added many more titles after this first group. The authors were all local art buffs, docents, or teachers from the Minneapolis Institute of Arts, the Walker Art Center, and the University of Minnesota. They included Joan Mondale, who wrote *Politics in Art.*

> " Lerner Publications has been important to the Mondales. Harry encouraged me to expand a slide talk, Politics in Art, into a book, which helped the public better understand the connection between the two. Thanks to Harry, I did write the book, and we are still proud of it. "
>
> *from* WALTER *and* JOAN MONDALE

POLITICS in art

The next step was to find a first-rate designer who would work on a very restricted budget. It so happened that one evening we attended a meeting of the Midwest Direct Mail Marketing group. The main speaker didn't show, so at the last minute, somebody scrounged up a substitute, a furniture designer who also designed a few brochures for the Walker Art Center.

His name was Robert Clark Nelson. As a lecturer, he didn't receive high marks. I even spotted a few people sleeping during his talk. But boy, was he creative! His slide show was so impressive that we immediately knew he had it in him to design our art books.

After some lengthy discussions about price, he agreed to do a sample mock-up. I still have it around some place. It was gorgeous—and only in two colors. Yes, an art book in two colors!

The first six books were two-color. They received numerous awards and got good reviews. They even won the prestigious Chicago Book Award for art design. (Robert eventually got tired of the project and had art students follow his designs on later volumes in the series.)

But we started to get complaints: no color. The sales reps and dealers said, "Who ever heard of an art book, let alone a series, without color?" But at the time, printing in color was expensive. Color separations were costly, much more so than modern scanning.

Okay, they wanted color—I'll give them some. We put four-page, full-color inserts into subsequent books. Eventually, we did twenty-one titles with inserts. I made sure we always flipped to the color pages first at the art and book shows where we exhibited.

Since the color separation and color printing were expensive, we devised ways to cut costs on other books. George Overlie was good at

Sharon and I were proud to display our art books.

this. He would do overlays on acetate or tracing paper for each color, avoiding the mechanical separation expense. But sometimes the colors didn't always fit. You could see the matching wasn't perfect. This was especially true of the Mr. Bumba books.

My good friend Leo Kibort was a partner in Green Printing, the least expensive printer in town, and he made us a deal. Instead of paying Green's strippers time and a half, Sharon and I used their prepress room in the evening. We opaqued and scratched film to get the colors to overlay perfectly.

We also tried to get the maximum advantage by overprinting two colors to get a third. One reference that was extremely helpful in this work was Donald Cooke's book *Color by Overprinting* (1955). This was a complete guidebook to art and printing techniques.

Anna's Art Adventure

CAROLRHODA LOCKETZ WAS A BUBBLY, PERKY GIRL who died too young. She was Sharon's best friend. Their mothers were close friends, and the two girls grew up together. They shared everything: stories, trips, and adventures. As students at the University of Minnesota, they spent a lot of evenings at the Ten O'Clock Scholar, a hangout on the West Bank of the university campus. They listened to the music of a young student dropout, Bob Zimmerman, later known as Bob Dylan.

While a university student, Carolrhoda worked part-time as a page at the Saint Paul Public Library. After graduation in 1962, she joined the Peace Corps. They assigned her to be a teacher-librarian in Harar, Ethiopia. Carolrhoda poured herself into the job and the people she worked with. She even set aside two hundred dollars of her own meager salary to create an educational fund for a twelve-year-old Ethiopian boy.

Peace Corps director Sargent Shriver, John F. Kennedy's brother-in-law, visited Harar when Carolrhoda was serving there.

*Carolrhoda and
a young friend in
Ethiopia*

*A Boy Named
Beckoning*

Carolrhoda met with Shriver and talked about the great need for books in Ethiopian libraries. He obviously listened because back in the United States he began a book drive for libraries everywhere Peace Corps volunteers served.

After returning to the United States, Carolrhoda married Gordon L. Rozell, an army sergeant she had met in Ethiopia. She died of cancer in 1967, two years after her marriage. She was only twenty-eight years old.

After Carolrhoda's untimely death, Sharon wanted to honor and pay tribute to her best friend, who was also Adam's godmother. So in 1969, we named the Carolrhoda imprint after her. It was a beautiful way to

The first books within the Carolrhoda imprint

immortalize Carolrhoda's memory in a manner that exemplified her love of books and learning. Sharon envisioned Carolrhoda books as attractive storybooks, heavily illustrated with art or photography. The first books were *This Is . . .* , a rhyming story for beginning readers, and *Have You Seen My Mother?*, the story of a brightly colored ball that searches for its mother at the circus.

The imprint was Sharon's hobby and passion, and she was thrilled each time a Carolrhoda book won an award or received a favorable review. Eventually, after Adam came on board, Carolrhoda became our trade imprint, and he added many new titles, including his first acquisition, the Little Wolf books by Ian Whybrow. I'm proud to say Carolrhoda is celebrating its fortieth anniversary this year.

> " I should like to thank Adam for taking on Little Wolf and introducing him to The Big Country in several languages. This is a kindness that the small brute appreciates as deeply as I, especially since he cannot spell and was nervous that his jokes might be lost on the American education system. The boy has penned a short ode: "
>
> *from* IAN WHYBROW

Arrrroooo for Adam Lerner
For pack-leadership plus punch.
Because if he likes your books a lot,
He takes you out to lunch.

And when he comes to London,
He shakes you by the paw
And makes you feel important
(That's what publishers are for).

He finds out what you're up to.
Then he'll pat your head and say:
"Well dun. Forget McDonald's;
We're off to The River Café!"

Arrrroooo for Adam Lerner
Plus fifty noisy cheers.
That's one for now and plenty
For another fifty years.

L. Wolf

Badness for Beginners

Little Wolf, Terror of the Shivery Sea

SHARON AND I WERE BOTH ACTIVE participants in the Minnesota Democratic-Farmer-Labor (DFL) Party, the state Democratic Party organization. We were always attending meetings, from the precinct level to the Minnesota state convention. I was a delegate during the heated Keith–Rolvaag gubernatorial campaign in 1966. I was the lone supporter of Karl Rolvaag when everyone else from our Plymouth delegation supported Sandy Keith. The convention was almost an all-nighter, going to twenty ballots. Although Keith won the DFL endorsement, Rolvaag won in the primary election. But he lost to Harold LeVander in the general election.

Although Sharon and I generally agreed politically, there was one exception. She opposed the Vietnam War from the very beginning. Initially, I wasn't sure about the war. I believed in the domino theory of Communism. At the time, this was Hubert Humphrey's position, and I always went along with Hubert.

In 1968 Sharon campaigned for Gene McCarthy vigorously. With a group of women, she went door-to-door, farmhouse to farmhouse, even passing out McCarthy literature in Wisconsin. Eventually, I

Sharon and I were big fans of Vice President Hubert Humphrey. Here we're with him at a fund-raiser for Minneapolis mayor Arthur Naftalin. We later published an adult biography about Hubert, called Undefeated.

came around to Sharon's point of view. Because I was so upset about the war, I even turned down an invitation to the White House to meet President Lyndon Johnson.

Here's what happened. In 1967 we published a book called *Polly and the President*. It told the story of a ten-year-old girl who visits the White House, gets lost, and ends up in the Oval Office with Johnson. The author, Mary Davis, contacted Minnesota congressman Don Fraser to arrange a presentation of her book to President Johnson.

> **"** I started work as an editor at Lerner in 1967. I entered publishing at a time of rising national turmoil, anguish, and transformation, and much of the work we did was driven by these changes. Immigration and ethnicity, economics, sex, protest movements—our subjects were all around us. **"**
>
> *from former Lerner editor* **MIRIAM BUTWIN**

Surprise of all surprises, the White House agreed and invited Mary and her publisher to Washington.

Mary flew to Washington and met with Johnson—she even had her picture taken with him and talked to him alone. Me? I told everyone within earshot, "I won't walk across the street to shake his hand" and stayed home in Minneapolis. Later, I could have kicked myself for passing up the opportunity to talk politics with Johnson.

In hindsight, Lyndon Johnson wasn't a bad president. Before he took office, only one-half of all public schools had libraries. When he left office, almost all public schools had libraries. This change was due to the National Defense Education Act (NDEA), which Johnson pushed through. It was an education bill to aid libraries. He tacked on the words "National Defense" to make it easier to get the bill through Congress. Lyndon Johnson, more than other presidents, was truly committed to improving schools.

*What DO Teachers Do
(after YOU Leave School)?*

HOW I GOT US OUT OF TROUBLE
IN VIETNAM

Ever since Mary's visit with Johnson, I've had this recurring dream that I too met with Johnson and spent some time discussing our headache in Vietnam. He was impressed with my knowledge of Asian land wars and the solutions I offered. He appointed me to create a think

THE PRESIDENT GETS A LERNER BOOK

Mary Davis with President Johnson

tank of my own gurus, i.e., buddies who were passionate about concluding the war and had the problem-solving skills necessary for such a task. I gathered this group together, and we flew to Hanoi (à la Henry Kissinger) and negotiated the settlement. (It was a far better deal than what we finally got.) And that's how I got us out of trouble in Vietnam.

EVERYONE SHOULD VISIT A WORLD'S FAIR at least once. This is what Sharon and I planned to do in 1967 when the fair—called the Montreal Expo—was held in Quebec. The fair was a mind-boggling combination of exhibits and pavilions from almost every country in the world. The theme was Man and His World, and attendance was reported at 50 million. We decided that August was a good time to go.

When preparing for the trip, we saw an enticing brochure advertising a new Montreal motel, the Canadiana. We mailed a deposit, and the motel reserved a room for us. But the motel turned out to be a temporary Quonset hut, with cardboard walls, a cheap bunk bed, and hardly anything else. "You call this accommodations!" I yelled at the manager. I asked for a return of our deposit, which he refused.

We then took a cab to the best hotel in town, the Queen Elizabeth, and they gave us a very nice room at virtually the same price. The manager at the Queen Elizabeth was sympathetic and said fair visitors shouldn't be taken advantage of. He had heard horrific stories of other travelers being cheated. I agreed and was determined to do something about the Canadiana. After all, no one likes to be ripped off.

Sharon, although hesitant, proved to be a good sport. She went along with my crazy idea of mounting a protest. Unfortunately, our protest caused more trouble than we had planned. A local art store sympathized with our protest. It gave us free art supplies so we could make signs. As we carried our handmade signs complaining about the motel, reporters and photographers gathered. The scene turned violent when one man, upset about being filmed, attacked one of the cameramen.

The news of our protest was broadcast all over Canada by English- and French-language newspapers, radio, and TV stations. Later, I learned the motel was part of a Mafia scam that involved shunting U.S. tourists by the hundreds to substandard facilities. The U.S. Post

This grainy photo is of the newspaper page showing Sharon and me in protest mode!

Office even returned mail addressed to the motel with *fraudulent* stamped on the envelopes.

> THE NEWS OF OUR PROTEST WAS
> BROADCAST ALL OVER CANADA.

Back in Minneapolis, booksellers from Toronto called me in amazement at what we had started, of course with a little giggle in their voices. I did feel a little guilty about the news cameraman being beaten up. I later used one of the pictures of the attack in our book *Freedom of the Press*.

I laugh every time I think of this incident. I'm not so sure I'd do the same thing today. Maybe I would!

Guan Yu

TO ME, IT NEVER MADE SENSE to pay others for renting space. I figured if the space is good enough for the landlords, then it's good enough for us.

Just do the math. Over time, in most cases, the rent you pay will cover the cost of the property. The mortgage payment often can be the same as the rent, sometimes less. Even if it's a little more, you're building equity in the property. The lesson here is one should own the building.

We had this little building at 133 First Avenue North for five years. We were rapidly outgrowing it. It had a total of six thousand square feet, including the basement. The first floor was my office and open space for Penny Moldo, the receptionist, plus one editor named Lynne Deur. The upper two floors were crowded by books and our packing area. We needed more space.

Almost every day I'd walk downtown to meet someone for lunch, go to the bank, and do errands. A block away, at 241 First Avenue North, I saw a For Sale sign. The building was called the Martin Building, named after the Martin brothers, who once manufactured children's

> **"** When I started at Lerner in 1964, the office was at another location on First Avenue. Often there were several winos propped up against the building ready to greet us. Harry and Penny shared the front office, and I walked through a warehouse space to a small secluded room that was the Lerner editorial office. **"**
>
> *from former Lerner editor* **LYNNE DEUR**

clothing under the name Klad-ezee Garments. I bought the building in 1966, and it still houses our editorial and production work. (By the way, one of the Martin brothers had a daughter who married Curt Carlson, who started his company, Gold Bond Stamps, in our building. There is a legacy here: the Radisson hotel chain, TGI Fridays, and Carlson Wagonlit Travel can all trace their origins to our 241 building.)

> **"** THEY SAY YOU SHOULDN'T LOOK BACK. BUT I CAN'T HELP MYSELF. I DO LOOK BACK, AND I KICK MYSELF EVERY TIME I THINK OF MISSED OPPORTUNITIES. **"**

All the real estate we own is related to or in close proximity to our business. But now I see how shortsighted I was. I could have

The left building, at 241 First Avenue North, houses our editorial, graphic design, IT, and contracts departments. The other building, the McKesson, is where our sales, marketing, and photo research departments do business. I have an office in the McKesson.

purchased more real estate at reasonable prices, but I was afraid the loans necessary to acquire more property would strap the funds needed for publishing books. I see now that I should have stretched and risked more to acquire adjacent buildings.

They say you shouldn't look back. But I can't help myself. I do look back, and I kick myself every time I think of missed opportunities.

Grandma Chickenlegs

Olive Wood

MY BROTHER AARON WAS A HOBBY CARPENTER. He had a complete carpentry workshop at home. He made chairs, tables, and small items such as pencil holders and decorative boxes. He liked woods and was knowledgeable about every type.

One year in the 1970s, Aaron volunteered to help set up the Department of Dermatology at the new medical school at the University of Beersheva in Israel. In Bethlehem he met an Arab antiques merchant who offered to sell him the trunk of an olive tree. Olive wood is beautiful and fun to work with, but it can be a challenge because it's very knotty.

The merchant offered to ship the trunk to Aaron in Connecticut after Aaron paid him in advance. Many months and many letters later, the trunk never showed up. Aaron even wrote to the Chamber of Commerce in Bethlehem. He never got an acknowledgment.

At the next Jerusalem Book Fair, Aaron asked me to check on the merchant to see what had happened to his olive trunk. Sharon and I and our friends Billy and Felicia Siegel drove down to Bethlehem to visit the antiques shop. The merchant remembered my brother and

Yale commissioned this painting of my brother Aaron.

acknowledged that he owed us a tree trunk and was prepared to give me one.

But how was I to carry a tree trunk? The merchant offered to cut it into blocks that measured about four by four by ten inches. He said twenty-two blocks equaled one trunk. "Okay," I said, "give me twenty-two blocks of olive wood." He said to come back in a couple of days and he'd have it ready.

I left Sharon at our stand at the fair and drove by myself in a small rented car. The merchant greeted me and gave me instructions, through small streets and alleys, to his garage. It took a while to find the place. When I arrived at the garage, a dozen young Arabs in their twenties were on guard. I popped the car trunk open and said, "Put it there."

They made several trips, carrying three or four blocks at a time, and gently laid them in the trunk of the car. They brought twenty blocks. "You're two short," I said. The leader of the group said, "The deal was twenty blocks."

The whole group of young men came closer and surrounded my car. I lit up my corona cigar and blew smoke at them. I wasn't sure who was more intimidated. I said I wasn't leaving until I got two more blocks of wood.

> I GAVE AARON TWENTY BLOCKS
> AND KEPT THE CONTROVERSIAL TWO,
> WHICH ARE STILL IN MY CLOSET.

My limited Arabic wasn't good enough, and I decided not to use Hebrew, fearing this might agitate them. They came closer, and I'm surprised today that I held my ground. I admit that I was a little nervous, and the thought crossed my mind that my obituary might appear silly. But my determination worked. The men went back into the garage and brought out two more blocks of olive wood. I gave Aaron twenty blocks and kept the controversial two, which are still in my closet. I don't think I'd do that today.

Here are the two blocks of olive wood I kept from Aaron's stash.

IN LATE 1977, Sharon was about seven months pregnant with Leah when we noticed a small lump, about the size of a nickel, in her right breast. No woman ignores a lump in her breast. We went immediately to her ob-gyn, who said it was probably a clogged milk duct. But to be sure, he suggested another opinion from a surgeon who would know better. The surgeon confirmed it was a clogged milk duct. Not to worry, the doctors said. After all, pregnant women don't get breast cancer.

After Leah's birth in January, Sharon wanted to breastfeed the baby as she had done with the other children. But the lump was still there. Sharon insisted on a biopsy. The pathologist at Mount Sinai Hospital said the tissue was positive for cancer. I didn't believe him. What happened to the clogged milk duct?

I immediately sent a slide to my brother Aaron at Yale Medical School to have their lab examine the tissue. Not only was the slide positive, but the cancer was very aggressive. Nodules had metastasized to her shoulder. Sharon was thirty-nine years old.

I commissioned the late Steven Rettegi to paint this portrait of Sharon.

The next year was no fun. After a mastectomy, chemotherapy and radiation followed. Loss of hair, loss of weight, and loss of energy took its toll. We were all nervous: her parents, her younger brother David, and her many friends. We had some good times, but in all, it was a four-year battle with many hospital stays. We always had a steady stream of visitors to the hospital, as well as to our house.

There was a period of re-mission, which we enjoyed. We took trips with the kids. The two of us flew the Concorde to London. We took a first-class trip around the world. Then the cancer returned.

We were all there at Methodist Hospital on March 8, 1982. Leah, age four; Danny, eleven; Mia, twelve; and Adam, fifteen. We didn't know it at the time, but our lives were changed forever. In the last hour, I asked Sharon not to leave us. I didn't know what to do with Leah, who was two months into her fourth year. Sharon said, "Don't worry. She'll turn out just fine." Her last words were the Shema, a traditional Hebrew prayer.

Here's the family a couple of years after Leah, our youngest, was born.

Sharon had been our coach, our cheerleader, our crafts mother. She was the cement in our family. What do we do now? It was three days after my fiftieth birthday.

My mother-in-law insisted that Leah was too young to attend the funeral, and I wasn't sure what to do. I consulted Jerry Bach, a psychiatrist who knew our family. Jerry said not to leave Leah out of anything. Jerry was at the funeral and the gravesite. He monitored the kids not only at the cemetery but for weeks afterward. He insisted that Adam take up fencing to alleviate any hostility. His suggestions were very helpful.

I knew that stability was the most important thing to retain. The family was to stay together—the same house, the same schools, the

Vijay holds Leah in this family photo from 1982, the year Sharon died.

same routine as much as possible. We were fortunate in having a wonderful housekeeper, Vijay, who helped keep things together. But at the time, she didn't drive. So shopping and schlepping the kids to school, games, and friends' houses was left to me.

Although Vijay stayed for over a year, there were many times between housekeepers when I had to do everything: make the meals, the school lunches, and the beds; and take out the garbage. The best time of day was after ten or eleven at night, when the kids were in bed. If I wasn't doing midnight shopping at Byerly's, our all-night supermarket, I'd relax with a cigar while doing the dishes.

The older three kids went to the Saint Louis Park public schools. My second wife, Sandy, urged me to send Leah to Blake, a well-respected private high school. It was a better school.

*Ladybugs: Red, Fiery,
and Bright*

In Leah's senior year, every student had to make a presentation to the entire student body. Leah's topic was all the housekeepers we had had. She related how some just disappeared after complaining of too much work. Others took her to bars, even though she was only five. One had an addiction to Pepsi Cola and left bottles all over the house. The talk was a hoot and brought down the house. Danny videotaped the presentation. It is something to cherish.

Sharon made many miniature paintings, such as this potted plant from 1970.

Dandelions:
Stars in the Grass

Mark and Elizabeth

DURING SHARON'S ILLNESS, our publishing house was expanding. This was in no small part due to my nephew Mark, who was in charge of sales until 1991.

My wonderful assistant Elizabeth Petersen held things together in those years. Elizabeth was the most dedicated person any boss could ever hope to have. She spent long hours at the office, was obsessed with detail, attended many book fairs, and was knowledgeable about our business.

Let me tell you about Elizabeth. After attending Augsburg College, a Lutheran school in Minneapolis, she accepted a teaching position in North Dakota. After a year, when the job was not renewed, she came back to Minneapolis looking for work. Anything will do, she said. She took the only job we had, as a billing clerk. After a while, I noticed she was doing more—much more. On her own initiative, she would contact customers to increase their orders so they would qualify for greater discounts.

Elizabeth quickly rose within the company, becoming an editor and ultimately editorial director. She retired in 1988 after about twenty-two years, then went to work for Mark, who by that time had started his own publishing house, Oliver Press. Elizabeth died of uterine cancer and was mourned by all who knew her.

> **"** It was the early 1980s, and I'd worked full time at the company for a year or so. I felt pretty good about my job. Our extended family had adopted a saying first coined by Uncle Mendel. It was, "Get the dough." So one day, in Harry's office he asked, "When are you going to learn how to get the dough?" I laughed along with Harry, as that phrase boiled business down to the basics. I have kept it in mind ever since. **"**
>
> *from* **MARK LERNER**

> **"** Shortly after starting at Lerner in 1967, when I was typing invoices on a manual Royal typewriter that had been electrified and sounded like a jackhammer, Harry called me into his office. He gave me a business-card size piece of stiff white paper on which he had hand lettered in india ink the words, "Sell Books." "Always remember," he said, "that's what this business is all about." **"**
>
> *from the late* **ELIZABETH PETERSEN**

BOOK FAIRS ARE FUN, but they are a lot of work. There must be hundreds of book fairs—from international exhibitions to local community fairs. There are specialized fairs for antiquarian booksellers, small press fairs, and remainder fairs. There are a zillion school book fairs, and we attend many of them. With LernerClassroom, we attend a lot of educational fairs.

I like the big fairs best. They get my adrenaline going. The two big domestic fairs are BookExpo America (BEA) and the ALA annual conference. For publishers, the exhibits are the attraction. This is where you meet customers, dealers, sales reps, authors and illustrators, and would-be authors and illustrators. Both ALA and BEA have certain hours for the trade and separate hours for the general public, usually weekends. Many book fairs host special programs and seminars. Our editors often attend these events, and this learning experience can be most helpful.

In the early days, we could afford only a single booth, usually ten feet long. I can't count the number of times Sharon, Elizabeth, and I set up and tore down exhibits on our own. It took me twenty-five years

How things have changed! Above is our stand in the 1970s. At right is our island stand that we use at the big shows.

of ALA and BEA before I gave up this work. Our company has grown to three or four booth spaces at most shows. For the bigger shows, we even have a twenty-foot by thirty-foot island with signage that you can see from far away. Others on our staff now do the setting up and tearing down. I must admit, I don't miss that part.

The international fairs are the most interesting for me. The Frankfurt Book Fair is the big one. The Bologna International Fair is also important because it is the world's top children's book fair. I have cultivated many friends exhibiting at these fairs for so many years.

> ❝ At my first participation to the Frankfurt Book Fair in 1976, Sharon Lerner was waiting for me with *Nature Album* for children on display at our stand. That was the start of my work with Lerner Publishing Group. We've enjoyed a close relationship and friendship with the Lerners since then. Congratulations! ❞
>
> *from* **AKIKO KURITA,** *Japan Foreign-Rights Centre*

We were the first U.S. publisher to have a separate stand at Bologna. I forget the year, but it was the mid-1960s. The other U.S. publishers were showing their books in a combined exhibit. At our first Bologna fair, we acquired four books from Iran, from a company called Intellectual Development for Children, which was owned by the wife of the shah. They sent us film and rough translation from Farsi, which we heavily rewrote.

In addition to Frankfurt and Bologna, I've attended book fairs in Jerusalem (a lot of fun); Moscow (you had to be careful not to offend the Communist regime's censorship rules); Warsaw, Poland; London, England; Guadalajara, Mexico; and Harare, Zimbabwe. I'm really a book fair junkie. I keep imagining that if I ever retire, I'll just go from one fair to another. Some day I'd like to go to the Beijing, Bangkok, and Australian fairs.

The Clock Struck One

MEETING PRIME MINISTERS

Every time we exhibit at the Jerusalem Book Fair, Israel's prime ministers come by our stand to look over our books. I always take the opportunity to talk with them and occasionally to have my picture taken with them. By the way, Yitzhak Rabin wanted to see the exhibits, but he arranged to come to the fair at two in the morning! I don't think I ever met him.

With Shimon Peres (left) *and Yitzhak Shamir* (below)

Sandy snapped this photo of me with Sheikh Hamdan bin Zayed Al-Nahyan, one of the country's leaders, at the Abu Dhabi International Book Fair. He was a very friendly guy.

Not long ago, I read about an interesting fair in Abu Dhabi. My wife Sandy and I decided to attend in March of 2008. To get there, we flew over Iraq, hoping that no heat-seeking missiles were out and about that night. The book fair was held in a brand-new hall called the New Exposition Center, and we were the only U.S. publisher to have our own stand.

Because all students in the United Arab Emirates are taught in English, our books were a big hit and we sold all that we brought. The sheikh, whom we met at the fair, had given all schoolkids a voucher to buy a book. Even more impressive, most educators had big sacks full of coupons, in some cases worth thousands of dollars. When all was said and done, we felt the Abu Dhabi International Book Fair was one of the most colorful and fascinating we'd ever attended, and we were glad to have experienced it.

I ONCE HEARD SOMEONE SAY that "book publishing is nothing more than the buying and selling of ideas." That's not only simplistic and cute, it's true. Publishers purchase an idea from an author in book form, then go out and market the book. Isn't that what was just said?

Once a manuscript lands on the publisher's desk, quite a few things need to happen. Let's say the publisher likes the idea and wants to publish the book. Either the publisher or someone important in the company will read the manuscript to determine how much editorial work is needed. Figuring out how much work to do is a tricky job.

We test applicants for editorial positions on their knowledge of grammar, sentence structure, and general information. We also give them a geography test to see how many countries they can identify on a world map. I'm always surprised that many cannot find India or France.

Our editors enjoy their jobs. Lee Engfer, who worked for us for many years, said that "working at Lerner was like being in elementary school again—we cut and pasted pictures, looked things up in the *World Book Encyclopedia*." She added, "After editing books about subjects from Dwight Eisenhower to trompe l'œil painting, I know a little bit about practically everything (which comes in handy at parties)."

> WE TEST APPLICANTS FOR EDITORIAL POSITIONS ON THEIR KNOWLEDGE OF GRAMMAR, SENTENCE STRUCTURE, AND GENERAL INFORMATION.

We've had many editors who were brilliant academically. They were at the top of their classes in college. They had advanced degrees, yet they never really understood our market or the reading skills of children. They simply weren't smart enough to get it. Or maybe they were too smart to get it!

The best editors are not only skillful at their craft but can be counted on to build a good relationship with authors. Often an editor will spend a lot of time with an author, listening to his or her problems and anxieties. The editor becomes the mentor, the parent, and the hand-holder to the author.

In some cases, the relationship becomes so thick that when the editor leaves the publishing house, he or she convinces the author to come along. This happens a lot in the New York publishing scene. To me, this doesn't pass the smell test. It seems like a form of theft. Fortunately, it hasn't happened to us that I'm aware of.

Rainbow Soup

IN THE 1990S, JUDY WILSON WAS PRESIDENT and general manager of the Macmillan Children's Book Group. I always admired her approach. She had separate managers for each of the ten imprints Macmillan had at the time. Each manager had a great deal of independence in structuring his or her list. Each had the authority to make most decisions regarding staffing, paying authors, and even marketing. Sometimes problems arose when managers competed with one another for the same author and subject. There were competitions within the house but not so severe as to bring about significant problems. In fact, competition often brought out the best.

Some publishing houses have one editor in chief, responsible for the entire list—for all the series and for all the major decisions. I prefer having separate managers. We've tried it both ways. In 1998, around the time Adam joined the company, we restructured our editorial group to bring all the editors and editorial managers together. At that time, we had quite a few unpublished manuscripts—some of them had been with us for years. We needed to decide what to do with the old acquisitions and figure out in what direction to take our imprints

> **66** How could I possibly express how much pleasure Lerner provided me in the year that I spent shuttling back and forth between New York and Minneapolis? Harry has built Lerner Publishing Group into a magnificent and highly respected company, and I will always appreciate the chance to contribute to it for a short time. **99**
>
> *from the late* JUDY WILSON

Jackson and Bud's Bumpy Ride

for the future. Managing editors were responsible for the day-to-day oversight of bringing books from manuscript to printer. It didn't matter which imprint was involved. But we really had only Carolrhoda and Lerner to worry about.

Then, in 2004, we bought Millbrook Press and Twenty-First Century Books. These imprints brought a lot of new books into our list. We took a good look at the hundreds of titles all the imprints had published over the years. We defined each imprint and moved books around among imprints where we saw the best fit. You wouldn't believe how long this took!

Stop and Go, Yes and No

STOP

GO

" The van Tulleken Company, which represented Millbrook during its sale to Lerner, has had the pleasure of knowing both generations of Lerners. Harry, the gutsy pioneer who built a highly successful, independent publishing company, and Adam, a true visionary who is taking Lerner to even greater heights. The business that we sold them is, as expected, thriving exceptionally well under their able tutelage. Congratulations on 50 years—an extraordinary milestone for two extraordinary men. "

from ROBIN WARNER, managing director of the van Tulleken Company

By 2006 Adam and editor in chief Mary Rodgers were ready to go back to an imprint-driven model. So now we have editorial directors in charge of imprints. But we still have one editor in chief.

Ruby Valentine

BOOK PUBLISHERS MEET THE STRANGEST ASSORTMENT of people who want to write books. They all have an interesting story to tell and want to tell it to every potential publisher. We usually reject their ideas simply because they don't fit our market; we could not do justice to the stories. And in most cases, these potential authors don't write well. We'd be stuck putting an inordinate amount of editorial time into their manuscripts. Sometimes the authors want too much money. Here are a few examples from my early days in publishing.

In 1967, about fifteen years after the Korean War, a young man came to visit me. He was pleasant but nervous. It was obvious that he had a blue-collar background, barely a high school education. His last name was Tennison. He wanted to tell his story. It seems that during the Korean War, he had been taken prisoner by the Chinese. Afterward, he had stayed in China. He was assigned to work in a factory, learned the language but not well, and was given a decent apartment. After a dozen years of this life, he left and somehow found his way back to Minnesota.

I listened to his story, until it became obvious that he was still a committed Communist. He was one of about a dozen U.S. soldiers who had refused repatriation, preferring to stay in the Communist system. Clearly they had been brainwashed. They believed everything about our capitalist economy was bad. They wanted to stay in China and help build a Socialist order, where equality reigned. This man's book would find no home on our list. I don't know if he ever had it published.

Another visitor had another war story—this time about World War II. He had been among the first soldiers to reach Hitler's Bavarian headquarters in Berchtesgaden. There, he came upon the photo studio of Hitler's personal photographer, Heinrich Hoffmann. He found a number of canisters of black-and-white, 35mm film. He stuffed them in his saddlebag.

Twenty-five years later, finally going through his old army gear, he found the canisters. They should have been turned in to the U.S. Army years before. But by then he figured they were his. He had the negatives developed and found pictures of Hitler in various poses. Some were candid shots, never seen before.

The ex-GI wanted to sell the photos for a steep price. I showed them to University of Minnesota professor Harold Deutsch, a well-known expert on Germany and World War II. Dr. Deutsch thought the photos were certainly rare, especially some that showed Hitler wearing glasses. Hitler wouldn't wear glasses in public, because to him the glasses demonstrated a physical weakness to which he would never admit. I passed on this project because the ex-GI wanted too much money. I also worried that I could be prosecuted for acquiring contraband material.

Once, an elderly European man with a thick Slavic accent came by. He wore a large black leather coat. He, too, wanted to tell me his story. He had been born in Poland. As a student at the Warsaw University in the 1930s, he became very active in the Communist Party. He became so caught up in Communist ideology that he transferred to the University of Moscow. In the late 1930s, Stalin carried out his Great Purge, eliminating all persons considered disloyal to the Soviet Union. The purge included all foreigners in the USSR, whom Stalin thought were foreign agents. The man who came to see me was tried and sent to a Siberian gulag, where he spent the World War II years as a prisoner. He would not tell me how he escaped, except to say it was through Siberia to Asia. It's a mystery to me how he got out.

> **I KNEW FOR SURE THAT I DIDN'T WANT TO BOTHER WITH ANTI-SOVIET HUMOR.**

What did he want to write about? Not his experience in the gulag. No—he wanted to publish a book of anti-Communist, anti-Soviet humor! He was a funny man with funny stories, and he thought his comic sketches would find an audience in the United States. I wasn't so sure that a U.S. audience wanted to bother with anti-Soviet humor. But I knew for sure that I didn't want to bother with anti-Soviet humor. I don't know if his stories were ever published.

One of the most familiar photographs of the Holocaust is of a little boy surrounded by German soldiers. He has his arms raised and a machine gun pointed at him. Did this boy survive the war?

Sometime in the 1980s, an article appeared in the *London Jewish Chronicle* about a man claiming to be the kid in the photo. The reporter who wrote the article made a convincing case. He said the man had pointed out several interesting features in the picture. Notice the crooked left thumb: "I was so hungry that I constantly sucked this thumb—so much that it became very sore. And do you see the collar of my coat? That is where my mother had sewn a couple of gold coins."

This photo was taken as part of the Nazis' documentation of their suppression of the Warsaw ghetto uprising in 1943.

I assigned the reporter to investigate this man further and to write a book on the subject. The reporter began to discover holes in the man's story. He backed out of the assignment and returned the advance I had given him.

I wasn't ready to give up on the story so I checked with Yad Vashem, the Holocaust museum in Jerusalem. Yad Vashem said that many men claimed to be this boy. The museum had even dubbed him Dov. Then I ran across a video about another man, a Dr. Tsvi Nussbaum of New York, who also made the claim. I gave up searching for the boy. But that sure would have made a terrific book.

OF COURSE, WE'VE HAD A LOT OF SUCCESS with projects we did take on. One example that worked out well was with the author-illustrator Nancy Carlson. She first contacted us to offer her artwork, but we teamed her with editor Susan Pearson. Nancy and Susan developed stories about what became a whole neighborhood of characters, including Harriet, Walt, Louanne Pig, and Loudmouth George. The

first Nancy Carlson book we did was *Harriet's Recital* in 1982. We went on to publish many more.

We've sold thousands and thousands of copies of *Keep the Lights Burning, Abbie* which was originally published in 1985. Authors Peter and Connie Roop had been writing joke books for us. Then they sent in this serious manuscript about a real girl who kept the lighthouse lights burning during a serious storm in the late 1800s. Susan Pearson immediately saw the appeal of the story. It gave a new historical fiction thrust to our On My Own beginning reader series, which we started in 1979. *Reading Rainbow*, a children's PBS program to promote reading, picked up

> " When I first started publishing with Lerner, I was kind of scared of Harry. That was because I actually knew nothing about illustrating books, and I knew nothing about writing them!! I was sure Harry would soon figure that out! But instead, I found myself being encouraged to write not only one book, but a series of five, which were the Harriet books. I ended up writing sixteen books for Lerner in little over three years! It's pretty amazing Harry took such a chance with someone who had never even tried to write one book!! Later, Adam also took a chance on my work by redesigning all my old books. He also has since published some new ideas of mine. I want to thank Harry for giving me my start, and I want to thank Adam for his continued support. "

♡ *Nancy Carlson*
2008

the title, which no doubt accounts for its continued success. We've reprinted it nearly forty times, and it keeps selling!

I remember well the acquisition meeting where the editorial directors and I looked through the black-and-white photos taken by a medical doctor named David Parker. He had traveled to India, Nepal, Bangladesh, Indonesia, and Mexico to document the lives of working children. His images—from dust-covered kids working in stone quarries to tiny rug weavers with misshapen fingers—haunted us.

But no manuscript came with the images. Stacked unevenly in a box, they somehow seemed to tell their own story of the ravages of child labor. Editor Lee Engfer saw potential for a book and helped shape a story, illustrated with Dr. Parker's images, that became *Stolen Dreams*. In 1998 the book won the Minnesota Book Award and the Christopher Award for its effort to educate others about the dangers of child labor in the developing world.

Fact-checking is an editorial step we take with all our nonfiction books. But how can an editor tell if something is true or false in a personal memoir? In 2008, we published the picture book *Angel Girl*, which was a memoir of how Herman Rosenblatt survived a Nazi prison camp with the help of a girl on the outside, whom years later he met in New York on a blind date and married.

The book was beautifully illustrated by Ofra Amit, an Israeli artist. It was an incredible love story, so we thought. The author, Laurie Friedman, interviewed the couple, now in their late seventies, over and over again. They discussed every detail of the story and even went over all the art to ensure accuracy. The book came out to rave reviews. We printed "based on a true story" on the cover. "Incredible," however, turns out to be the operative word. Herman wasn't telling the truth about how he met his future wife. We immediately stopped selling the book and sent out a press release expressing our shock and sadness. It amazes me how someone could concoct such a story and stick to it for so many years.

ON A LESS SOMBER LEVEL, we also took a risk on books by a writer whose first offering came out of the slush pile—the unsolicited manuscripts that authors used to send to us. As a young editorial assistant, Martha Brennecke was charged with tackling our thousands of annual unsoliciteds. She found one that struck her funny bone. It was called *Jamaica Sandwich?*, a manuscript of punny verse by Brian P. Cleary. She pushed hard for approval of the acquisition. We published this title and three others in 1996, all illustrated by Rick Dupré.

Brian then sent Martha a new idea: books about the parts of speech, starting with a manuscript on nouns. Martha reminded Brian that we are a series publisher, so he immediately sent her manuscripts on verbs and adjectives. More experienced now, she developed the parts of speech series into a tight acquisition package. She thought it had possibilities as a long, successful series.

She approached Rick to do the artwork for all three books, with the idea of approximating a fad of the time called Claymation. Rick created many intricate statuettes that turned out to be incredibly

Here's a dummy spread of A Mink, a Fink, a Skating Rink, *with Rick Dupré's art in place. Note there are no cats. To the left is the final cover, with cats.*

labor intensive. Time was running out, and we were nowhere near getting the art done. Finally, Rick had to pull out. We needed a new artist FAST!

As it happened, we had a young assistant designer named Jenya Prosmitsky on staff who had gotten her art degree in Kishinev, Moldova, in the former Soviet Union. (Coincidence: that's where my father was born.) She had been showing around her portfolio, hoping to be considered for some freelance illustration. She did a sample, using her house cats as models. Bingo! Martha came up with the series name Words Are CATegorical.

So pick and fiddle, strum and stroke,

Tease and teeter,

Sob and soak.

Sweep your sidewalk

paint your curb,

And know each action is a Verb!

Hairy, Scary, Ordinary

What Is an Adjective?

by Brian P. Cleary
Illustrated by Jenya Prosmitsky

To Root, to Toot, to Parachute

What Is a Verb?

by Brian P. Cleary
Illustrated by Jenya Prosmitsky

Eventually, we hired staffer Jenya Prosmitsky, a young artist from Kishinev, to draw the art. She used her pet cats for inspiration, and the CATegorical franchise was the result.

Martha and then senior designer Zach Marell worked closely to envision the art for each spread of the first book *A Mink, a Fink, a Skating Rink: What Is a Noun?* They were going for wacky, slapstick humor, which they then explained to Jenya in detail so she could get it right. The pace was slow going. Enter Adam, who decided we should publish the books one at a time, starting in fall 1999. We've published at least one every year ever since! Librarians love them, and Brian has become a prolific author for us, working with many different editors and artists over the years. After illustrating three books, Jenya gave way to Brian Gable, a Canadian cartoonist.

Under, Over, By the Clover

On the Scale,
a Weighty Tale

Martha fired off the
first shots of this canon.
Ellen was helpful,
then Mary and Shannon
gave substance and strength
to an interesting series,
and Carol improved
all the "Brian P. Clearys."

Jenya created those
signature creatures
in whimsical places
with comical features.
Zach and his team
were the glue that would bind
the best-looking books
that were ever designed!

Brian P. Cleary, holding a copy of
A Mink, a Fink, a Skating Rink.
By the way, we are selling this
book in Britain but under the title
A Cat, a Bat, Your Grandma's Hat.
Seems the Brits didn't think their
kids would know what a fink was!

Once they were selling,
the art team was able
to enlist a cartoonist
whose name, Brian Gable,
was seen by adults
on their newspaper pages,
and now his cartooning
appeals to all ages!

Lazily, Crazily,
Just a Bit Nasally

Straight and Curvy,
Meek and Nervy

COMMUNIST EAST GERMANY had a propensity to change its language to fit its ideology. For instance, it eliminated the words *employer* and *employee* and called everyone workers. I rather like this equalizing wordage and use it once in a while.

The point here is that arrogance from supervisors is unwise. It's management's job to eliminate elitism. More than once, we've had workers switch jobs within the company for a few days. We've had editors work in the billing department and vice versa. We haven't done this for a while but should consider it again. Our managers will likely object, saying that the experiment will curtail efficiency and disrupt schedules. But in my opinion, it is worthwhile.

Before Adam came to our company, we were very skimpy on job titles. I personally never liked designating people by title. We didn't have vice presidents and other fancy titles. Often workers would ask for a title. I'd say, pick your own title, any title except president or publisher. But things change. As the company grew bigger, we had no choice but to conform to standard nomenclature. Adam designated a whole bunch of titles just like other companies have.

Adam and I pose with several of our vice presidents in around 2000. Seated next to me is Gary Hansen, who is also president of Interface Graphics and MBB. Behind him is David Wexler, executive vice president of sales. Next to David is Margaret Wunderlich, executive vice president and CFO. Mary Rodgers, vice president and editor in chief, is next. The woman behind Adam, Beth Heiss, was once our marketing director but is no longer with the company.

We are very fortunate to have many long-term employees on staff. I'm especially proud of Cully, Billie, and Gary, who have been with us for well over thirty years, as well as Marlene Ferrel and Ada Wasserman.

Colleen (Cully) Gafny took a business preparation class in high school and after graduating joined us as a receptionist. She did all the grunt work: answering the phone, making coffee, finding office supplies, and assisting editorial and marketing. She became our chief billing clerk. She's now customer service supervisor. She is proficient on the computer, knows where all the books are, keeps track of inventory, and fields every conceivable question about the status of every order. Since high school, she's never had another employer. The only thing she's changed is her last name—from Gafny to Cohen to Beisell. We all love Cully.

Cully celebrated her thirtieth anniversary with the company in 2002.

> “ In the early 1970s, I had the distinct honor of preparing HJL's coffee every morning. The oversized cup, filled two-thirds full at just the right temperature, awaited his arrival at 8:45 A.M. I find that a symbol of the quality and perfection that have continued on through the years. ”
>
> *from* COLLEEN BEISELL

I'm proud to have someone as dedicated as Billie Sibley (right) *on our staff.*

At the age of eighteen, Billie Sibley moved to Minnesota from rural Mississippi. She had been picking cotton from the time she was able to walk to the age of eighteen, when she figured there had to be more than that to life. She left her family and moved to Minneapolis, where she found work in our shipping department. She's been with us over thirty years, still packing, still applying postage. She knows the location of every book in our warehouse.

Billie is the only one left who remembers the transformation of our warehouse and shipping department. When she first came here, she worked in the basement shipping department of the 241 building, which was cold in the winter and sweltering in summer. Later, the department moved to the upper floor of the McKesson Building, still cold in winter and hot in summer. And working in a multifloor building, moving books up and down a freight elevator, wasn't easy.

Now we have a modern warehouse, complete with the latest conveyors and digital apparatuses. Billie has experienced it all.

I'm proud of Billie and we all appreciate her good nature. She gave us the "Billie Rule," by which employees can withdraw funds from the company profit-sharing plan before retiring.

I've always boasted that Gary Hansen is the most knowledgeable book production person around. He started out in our prepress department more than thirty-five years ago. He is now president of Interface Graphics, Inc., our production division, and MBB. He oversees all our book production—from purchasing paper and printing to manufacturing books for ourselves and others. Our companies have been lucky to have Gary's knowledge and leadership to turn to in an extremely challenging environment for book manufacturing. Gary also serves on our company investment committee. He has great judgment when it comes to people, expenses, and finances.

> " I started working at Lerner Publications in 1973. It was a small, stable company that had two imprints, Lerner and Carolrhoda. The Lerner catalog had 240 titles, and Carolrhoda had 39. We published 35 new titles my first year. In 2007, we published 366 titles. Like Harry always says, "Never Enough Books." "
>
> *from* GARY HANSEN

Business Plans and Budgets

IT SEEMS THAT EVERYONE who wants to start a new business talks about developing a business plan. Maybe they teach that in Business 101 at college. Frankly, I had never heard about such a thing when I started our company.

My business plan was an idea—combined with confidence, shrewdness, good luck, hard work, and many long hours. My favorite three words for success are *tenacity well directed*, which sort of tells it all.

The word *budget* has always bothered me. Accountants and bookkeepers like to see every expense planned and accounted for. Big corporations like HarperCollins and Random House have always concerned themselves with keeping within their budgets. To me, budgets are artificial rules. My mentor, Dave Boehm, said that budgets are more restrictive than helpful, especially for small businesses just getting started or expanding. If you have a good eye for cost effectiveness and are frugal, you don't have to be held back by budgets.

When interviewing prospective employees, I try to find out a little about their lifestyles. If they are naturally frugal and don't spend much on themselves, then they will also be cautious with spending company money.

> MY FAVORITE THREE WORDS FOR SUCCESS ARE *TENACITY WELL DIRECTED*, WHICH SORT OF TELLS IT ALL.

But another part of the question is that authors want to get paid. And publishers have to watch expenses. So how much is an author worth? That depends on the author. How good is she or he? Is the author known? Does she or he have a following? Does the manuscript require a lot of editing? Is an agent involved? Is the book an assignment or was it the author's idea? How is it to be illustrated—with art or with photographs?

In the early days before computers, we had no accurate method of keeping track of sales. So the simplest and most honest way to compensate an author was an outright purchase. If the author wouldn't agree to a purchase, I would offer to pay per printing. We paid directly from the printer's invoice. For instance, if we printed five thousand copies, we might pay twenty-five cents per book, or $1,250 each time the book went to press. The obvious advantage for the publisher was the small amount of bookkeeping and guaranteed accuracy.

Louanne Pig in The Talent Show

The disadvantage was paying for inventory that hadn't been sold yet and might never be sold in the quantities anticipated. Many times we sold out the first printing, reprinted, paid the author, and never sold much of the second printing. Publishers lose money on unsold books.

With computers, we can now determine with accuracy the royalties due on sales. And with the possibility of instant books and printing on demand, in some cases, lots of inventory isn't necessary.

How much do you charge for a book? All publishers have a discount schedule. The discount depends on the type of account: point-of-purchase (retailers), wholesale, or institution (schools and libraries). Quantity is always a factor.

On the Scale, a Weighty Tale

Here is one rule I've always kept in mind. Let's say you price the book at $20 and you're required to give a large purchaser 60 percent off. That means you're selling the book for $8. In this scenario, your manufacturing costs should not be more than one-half of that $8, or $4. So the book is marked up five times for a price of $20.

In many cases, you'll link with a much higher markup, like seven times. In other cases, such as with a heavily illustrated book, you'll be lucky to get a markup of three and one-half times. Try not to price your books too low, because you'll always have unanticipated expenses.

Many years ago, in the fifties, sixties, and seventies, school and library publishers had net prices. They gave a discount to schools and libraries but charged extra for the binding. The math looked like this: list price: $12.95; less 25 percent for a price of $9.71; reinforced binding: $5.00; final price: $14.71.

Most publishers stuck to this pricing system, but eventually the courts ruled that this was price fixing. A number of publishers were penalized with fines. Fortunately, at that time we were too small for anyone to bother with us.

WE NEVER QUIBBLE ABOUT SMALL THINGS.

Ever hear of a prebinder? These are distributors that are also bookbinders. Here is what they do: They purchase books from publishers, rip off the original covers, and replace them with their own covers, often made of tough buckram. Finally, they do their own reinforcing. They claim these books last longer and have greater circulation toughness than the original books. Sometimes this is true. Sometimes it is not.

It's not true compared to our Muscle Bound books, because our reinforced binding is as good as any. We guarantee these books forever. I don't think we get more than six complaints a year out of millions of books bound. In those rare cases, we'll either grant a credit or a replacement. We never quibble about small things.

ONCE UPON A TIME, there was a publisher named Franklin Watts. He was the originator of the series concept. Someone asked him: Why a series? His answer was simple and direct: To sell more books. If someone liked one book in the series, that person would likely buy more. Watts published "the first book of . . ." series, which included almost every subject imaginable.

Although I like publishing individual titles, our sales manager and school and library sales reps hate them. Obviously, the commission on a $500 series is greater than the commission on a single $19.95 book. The single title is never shown "first out of the bag," as we say. Many reps won't show customers a single title at all. I found this out early. Now when we do single titles, such as picture books, we try to bunch them together for selling purposes.

Here are some of the subjects we've tackled in series: economics, pollution, sports, sports cars, science fiction, crafts, animals, archaeology, karate, and social issues. We've expanded previously published series by adding new titles, and we've updated series upon reprinting.

In 1969, when new math was the rage in math education, we did a book on infinity, as well as books on one, zero, ten, etc. In 1969 our In America series (sample cover at right) included less-well-known ethnic groups to demonstrate that our country is a mosaic of cultures. In 1971 the Being Together series was the first of its kind covering human sexuality, with subjects ranging from circumcision to gender differences.

In the 1980s, we published ethnic cookbooks. We also acquired the Visual Geography Series from Sterling Publishing. This was a wonderful series but terribly out of date. All the pictures were black and white. We undertook a massive project to completely revise over one hundred titles, adding color, new statistics, and a new design. Mary Rodgers was in charge of this challenge. (In 2003 we started reissuing this series in full color, with new statistics and a new design.)

In 1991, when the Soviet Union collapsed, we were the first to publish a separate book on each of the newly created republics. The series was called Then and Now. Because getting current photographs was so difficult, we sent a young New York photographer to the former Soviet republics to take pictures for us. (Mary was also in charge of this series and loves to tell the story of the last manuscript arriving handwritten in Cyrillic!)

> **"** Everyone at Lerner has been delightful to work with, and the USA TODAY-branded books are sensational. Lerner Publishing Group is a forward-looking company that's well positioned to grow and thrive, but its roots are firmly planted in the small family company that it used to be. **"**
>
> *from USA TODAY editor* BEN NUSSBAUM

In the late 1990s, we made an arrangement with the Arts & Entertainment (A&E) Network to license the A&E name in biographies. This well-known *A&E Biography* television series added a lot of name recognition to our own biographies. Since then, we've negotiated publishing licenses with NASCAR® and USA TODAY®.

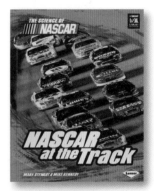

We also published a wonderful, fact-filled series called World in Conflict, covering areas like Rwanda, Sri Lanka, Bosnia, Haiti, and Sudan. It was a great disappointment to me when the series didn't sell well. I can't figure that one out. A wonderful list of books, perfect for social studies classes, just didn't find its way into schools.

We've also published many individual titles, including young adult novels. My brother Aaron wrote a book on Einstein and Newton—a comparison of the two greatest scientists. In the 1980s, one of our best sellers was *Fantasy Football Digest*. We sold about sixty-five thousand copies each year. The Web put this title out of business. Now, football statistics are available free and up-to-date online.

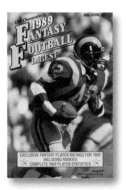

In our warehouse, we have a little room, organized by my son Danny, where we archive at least one copy of every book we publish. Sometimes I'll go in there just to look at what we've done. I'm truly amazed at the great variety of subjects we've published over the years. In fact, I can't think of a topic we haven't published.

> " Daily Printing, Inc. first started its partnership with Lerner Publishing Group in 1994. At that time, we produced book covers for the annual *Fantasy Football Digest*. The business has grown since then, and Lerner is one of our top customers. We print thousands of texts and covers for the company. Thank you for the business, and we look forward to working with Lerner the next fifty years. "
>
> *from* R. PETER JACOBSON, *president, and*
> JOHN MANUEL, *senior account manager,*
> *Daily Printing, Inc.*

PEOPLE OFTEN ASK ME to name my favorite Lerner books. That's like asking about your favorite finger or your favorite child. By the time this book has been published, we will have published perhaps ten thousand titles, including acquisitions.

A few of these books stand out or mean something special to me. Many of them are out of print today. (By the way, I don't like using the word *today* in our books because it limits their longevity. I often remind editors to avoid certain words and have occasionally passed out this forbidden word list: *today, currently, now, at this time, presently, nowadays, recently, coming soon.* I know I've used these words a lot in this book, but hey, it's a memoir!)

Red Man, White Man, African Chief (1960), by my sister-in-law Marguerite Rush Lerner, is one favorite book. It offers a scientific explanation of why human skin comes in different colors. By providing a scientific explanation, the book helped readers think

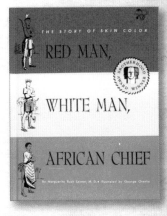

Spring is awaking.
She touches the apple tree.
The first green leaves wait for more.

differently about people of different races.

Who Will Wake Up Spring (1967) (sample spread at left), by Sharon Lerner, features a beautiful collage of a tree whose leaves change throughout the year.

Another favorite is *The Whistle* (1974), by Benjamin Franklin, illustrated in a woodcut style by George Overlie. Whenever I've paid too much for something, I think about Ben Franklin's words, "He paid too much for his whistle."

The Girl Who Owned a City by O. T. Nelson (1975) is a thrilling tale of children who inherit the world after a devastating catastrophe. This is an example of an author who has only one good book in him. Nelson wrote other manuscripts, but they just didn't measure up to his first one. To my knowledge, they weren't published, at least not by us.

The Cigarette Sellers of Three Crosses Square (1975) by Joseph Ziemian is the astonishing true story of a group of Jewish children who managed to escape from the Warsaw ghetto in 1942 and survive in the Aryan section of the Nazi-occupied city. The kids sold cigarettes to German soldiers, passing themselves off as non-Jewish. A map in the book shows where the cigarette sellers worked. In 1995, when I attended the Warsaw Book Fair, I located the entire neighborhood. Most of the streets were exactly as they had been in 1944. It was exciting to walk the same streets the kids had many years before under the worst possible circumstances.

Another standout is *A Migrant Family* (1991) by Larry Dane Brimner. It takes a sympathetic look at how poor migrant workers try to eke out a living. The social message is powerful. Another is *Laurie Tells* by Linda Lowery (1994). This book has special meaning not only for its traumatic story about child abuse but also because it's the last book I personally designed. I directed the artist to increase the size of the artwork sequentially, from small to large to larger at the end of the book. I felt the story called for this dramatic approach.

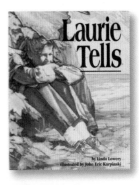

My favorite series are Visual Geography, Pro/Con, and World in Conflict. VGS has sold extremely well, in many editions. The other two series didn't do as well. Their sales were a disappointment to me, as they are excellent books.

If you asked Adam, he'd probably mention titles that have received major awards. The picture book *Almost to Freedom* won a Coretta Scott King Illustrator Honor in 2004.

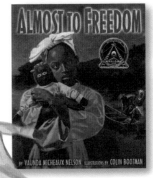

" A meaningful moment of my twenty-year partnership with Lerner occurred at an ALA in New Orleans. There, Adam said that winning the Sibert only confirmed how committed he, his family, and the company—employees and authors—are to creating excellent children's literature. That's when I truly felt part of the Lerner family. "

from SALLY M. WALKER

" I am gob smacked by what Lerner has achieved in the last fifty years, perhaps even more so in the last ten. From its place as a reliable, steady series publisher, Adam has forged a new, quality publishing house that is winning awards and impressing the heck out of its audience. "

from KATHLEEN BAXTER,
nonfiction columnist for School Library Journal

Secrets of a Civil War Submarine: Solving the Mysteries of the H. L. Hunley by Sally M. Walker received the coveted Robert F. Sibert Informational Book Medal in 2006. She followed up that book with *Written in Bone*, which came out to coincide with a Smithsonian exhibit of the same name.

AUDIO BOOKS HAVE ALWAYS BEEN POPULAR. First they were on records, then eight-track devices, then cassettes, and now disks. They can be downloaded to iPods. Audio books are particularly popular with drivers who travel long distances. Listeners can get their favorite authors and stories delivered right to their ears without reading a word.

But what if you could bypass the ears and go directly to the brain? Just imagine students and everyone else directly absorbing knowledge. You could do this while sleeping. You'd wake up with far more knowledge than you had before going to bed. Sounds futuristic? Maybe not.

I think the "reading and listening bypass machine" will someday come into being. Wouldn't this be something!

This is my own drawing of the bypass machine.

PRACTICALLY EVERY ASPECT of book publishing has changed drastically since 1959. Has anyone today ever heard of carbon paper, monotype machines, micrographs, spirit duplicators, slide projectors, a watts line, or an Elliott addressing machine? How about keyline boards, color keys, chromolins, or dyluxes? Probably not. We no longer use film and typesetting machines. Now it's all done on computer.

I admit to being old school. Even though I see the ease of the new technology, I miss the hands-on fun. I can't remember all the details of going electronic. So I asked several longtime employees about it.

Mary and Vicki, both in editorial, remember when we had one computer station that all the editors had to use. They signed up for a time slot and brought their floppy disks to the workstation. The manuscripts, by the way, often arrived typed on a typewriter. Some even came handwritten! We had a person on staff whose sole job was to retype these manuscripts on a computer, so we'd be able to edit them electronically. To typeset a book, we sent the disk to an outside company, which sent back camera-ready galleys called RCs. Any corrections had to be sent back to the typesetting company for new RCs to be made. The backs of the final RCs were then waxed—we had our own waxer at least—and then designers meticulously stuck the galleys on keyline boards.

Zach, Jim, and Gary remember the good old days too . . . before computers and direct-to-plate printing. Zach recalls how he'd use rub-down letters and the copy machine to create chapter headings. Sometimes this could take him half a day. He and Jim also created thumbnails—remember them? These are tiny versions of page layouts. The designers used them as a guide for how they'd lay out the whole book on keyline boards.

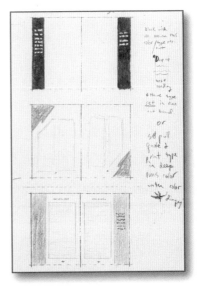

Above: *A designer's thumbnail.* Below: *A keyliner affixes type to a keyline board.*

After the keyline boards were final, they went into our stripping department. We had huge cameras in-house that shot the boards and prints to make film. We paid separation houses to separate color slides into the four color layers—cyan (C), magenta (M), yellow (Y), and black (K). Strippers like Gary used the film to build an orange flat of each signature. Any corrections meant we created new film. Strippers carefully registered the films and then secured them

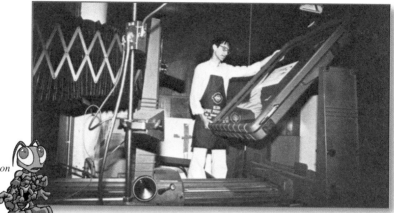

Alien Incident on Planet J

We had huge in-house cameras that shot keyline boards and photos.

When Gary Hansen first started working for our company, he was a stripper. Here he's stripping film negatives into a flat.

to the orange flat with ruby lith tape. We'd keep working films and send the printer dupe films of the flats. That's a lot of film!

Our designers didn't start using Macs for desktop publishing until around 1994. Zach recalls the first Mac was a Centris 610. Designers got on-the-job training an hour a day by signing up to use this machine. That was it. Within a year or so, each designer had a Mac. Then

EXTRACTING SILVER

Every piece of film we processed had silver in it, and we were processing a lot of film in those days. We hooked up with a recycler to extract the silver. Every stripper saved any rejected film in big barrels. When we had eight or ten barrels of old film, the recycler would collect them and weigh them. Instead of cash for the silver he'd extracted, we'd get silver ingots. Another extraction came from the fixer liquid. It contained silver too. Magnetized paddles constantly stirred the fixer and would attract any extra silver. Every few months, one of the strippers would remove the paddles now caked with silver. They'd chisel off the silver in thick flakes, and the recycler would create bars or coins. I'd give some of them to employees as gifts.

we started moving from stripping film to Mac-based prepress work. That added several more Mac users. Editorial created the job of production editors, who were also on Macs. (By this time, editors each had their own PC for editing manuscripts, and we made it part of our author contracts that manuscripts had to be delivered on disk.) By around 2000, all PCs and Macs were networked. We now send printers an electronic file. No film necessary!

The borders of this new universe are still unclear, and they are constantly being redefined. These days, we have print on demand, which has changed how publishers keep their inventory. On the retail level, we used to sell to ma and pa bookstores. Now chains dominate the landscape. On the educational front, schools no longer refer to libraries as such but rather call them media centers. Computers, iPods, and electronic gadgets line the desks of schools and libraries.

The camaraderie among publishers has also changed. Competition is fierce. Independent publishers used to share ideas. Now major corporations vie for market share. Survival of the fittest is the rule, not only in book publishing but in industries across the nation and on other continents as well. Some will say this competitive atmosphere has always been the case. But from my experience, this was not always true.

I am excited about a new invention, the Espresso Book Machine. It is able to print a three-hundred-page book economically, either one at a time or in small quantities. This device eliminates the large distribution warehouses that publishers have needed. From a bookstore or a home computer, readers can order from millions of titles.

Druscilla's Halloween

Sandy

IT WAS JANUARY 13, 1998. The anesthesia was wearing off. I had just gotten out of surgery. I had had a triple heart bypass at Abbott Northwestern Hospital in Minneapolis. Unknown to me, my attendant was to be a male nurse.

They were all there—Sandy and my four kids. In the recovery room, Sandy spotted a very attractive nurse attending other patients. Knowing me well, she asked the manager to switch nurses, so that I would wake up to this nurse's beautiful face. This will tell you something about Sandy. She has a sense of style like no other. And a sense of humor.

I first met Sandy on Christmas Eve 1985. I was invited to a dinner party at a friend's house with three other couples. (There's not much for Jews to do on Christmas, so we either have parties at home or go to Chinese restaurants.) Sharon had passed away in 1982, and I was starting to date.

Sandy came to the dinner party late because she had to work that day. She is a church organist, and Christmas Eve is a big deal at the Chapel Hills United Church of Christ in Edina. Sandy has been

Sandy and me relaxing

playing the organ at this church since 1969. She loves that congregation, and they love her.

Sandy and I were seated next to each other and sparks flew. We dated for a long time, started sharing living quarters in 1990, and finally got married in 1996.

Sandy is a remarkable woman. She first married at the age of nineteen. She had three kids, a girl and two boys. She now considers Leah

her fourth, since she came into our lives when Leah was so young.

Sandy is a voracious reader. She often reads four books simultaneously, in addition to proofreading many manuscripts for our company. She has a memory for dates and places like no other person. And she's been a world-class speller since grade

Used Any Numbers Lately?

Sandy and I are all decked out for a party for Elie Wiesel.

school. She was the Duluth spelling bee champion for three years in a row, starting at the age of eleven. She has a master's degree in English history and almost but not quite a PhD in Russian studies from the University of Minnesota. Sometimes I'll quiz her on exactly when Napoleon entered Vienna or about a specific incident in Victorian England. Obscure facts are her specialty. We once discussed the difference between a musket and a rifle.

This is Sandy—full of facts and fun. She's unflaggingly charming to those who are bright and a little less tolerant of those who are not. Her manner is cool. She oozes self-confidence and a sophisticated sense of humor. She's flirtatious and generally prefers males to females. She has a taste for clothes. Lots of clothes. I even had to convert an extra bedroom into a closet for her wardrobe. She's loving, a good stepmother and grandmother, and we have lots of fun together.

All Year Long

ONE QUICK WAY OF EXPANDING a list, as well as a quick way to introduce new and unique art and subject matter to a list, is acquiring books from foreign countries. We often do this at the Frankfurt and Bologna book fairs. We have also acquired series of books from other U.S. publishers, namely the Hammond Map Company, Stein & Day, and Sterling Publishing.

Acquiring outside companies has also allowed us to expand substantially. Other than our first acquisition of Muscle Bound Bindery, we have made three more worth mentioning: Interface Graphics, Inc. (IGI), Kar-Ben Publishing, and Millbrook Press. The first two just fell into our laps.

Typesetting was always a major expense. We were constantly being hit with extra charges for inevitable changes and corrections. I felt the typesetters were gouging us on additional costs beyond their original quotes. At one time, we were spending in excess of two hundred thousand dollars a year on typesetting.

Then, in the summer of 1994, Kathy Raid paid us a call. Kathy owned a small typesetting company in Minneapolis that was in desperate need of work. She had an office in the Ford Centre Building and quoted us some very competitive prices. She had a small staff and depended upon a young student at the University of Minnesota to keep her machines in good working order. (This student, Robert Stevens, went on to form his own company, the Geek Squad, which became the country's largest computer repair firm and is now owned by Best Buy.) Kathy offered to sell Interface Graphics to us with the understanding that she would continue running it.

Above: *A typesetter at work in the early 1980s. Note the huge floppy disks and the clunky monitor.*
Below: *Huge machines in our prepress area churn out proofs of our books before they go to the printer.*

Kathy's equipment was becoming antiquated as newer and faster computers were being developed. We upgraded the equipment and added a number of machines. Kathy and her partner, Lenny, worked for us for several years. Today IGI is a modern prepress operation. It handles all the design, prepress work, photo research, and production checks for our books, as well as that of some other companies.

On to our second acquisition. Two very bright and talented ladies, Judye Groner and Madeline Wikler, owned Kar-Ben Publishing in Rockville, Maryland. They specialized in children's books for the Judaica market.

After twenty-five successful years, Judye and Madeline thought it was time to sell their company. They sent Adam a large selection of their books. Adam's first instinct was to send them back without closely examining them. About a week after they were returned, he reconsidered. He requested the box of books again.

Acquiring Kar-Ben had many advantages. The books were good, and the imprint had a wonderful reputation in the Judaica market. Our decision was to purchase the company. In doing so, we acquired a profitable customer for both IGI and Muscle Bound Bindery. This happened in the winter of 2001–2002. Immediately after the sale, we moved the inventory to Minneapolis and eventually

Nachshon, Who Was Afraid to Swim

> "Kar-Ben has flourished under the Lerner umbrella, and we have enjoyed working with the dedicated professionals who help design, market, and sell our books."
>
> *from* JUDYE GRONER *and* MADELINE WIKLER

Kate Shelley and the Midnight Express

closed the Rockville office. Both parties were pleased. Another win-win situation.

Millbrook Press of Brookfield, Connecticut, had three divisions, all of which enjoyed a reputation for high quality and good reviews. Their imprints were Millbrook Press for elementary schoolchildren, Roaring Brook Press for the trade, and Twenty-First Century Books (TFCB) for middle school, high school, and junior college.

The books were editorially and artistically well done, but the company was poorly managed financially. Millbrook was a publicly held company that was rupturing cash like crazy. Eventually, because the company was forced to file for bankruptcy, it was up for grabs. First, Holtzbrinck bought Roaring Brook.

We put in a bid for the remaining parts, Millbrook and TFCB. The bankruptcy court accepted our bid, and we thought we had the deal sewed up. Then, at the last minute, a competing publisher pulled a nasty surprise. It made another offer, undercutting our bid. I was extremely upset because this competitor was a fellow Minnesota company. Millbrook was thrown into an auction. We met with the bankruptcy court in New York and finally prevailed in the bidding, paying over twice our original offer.

At first it was difficult absorbing Millbrook. It had substantial inventory in the Simon & Schuster warehouse in Pennsylvania that had to be moved. We rented additional warehouse space in Minneapolis. We eventually closed the Brookfield office but retained Millbrook's president, Jean Reynolds, as an executive editor for a few years. (She retired in 2008 but still works with us on a freelance basis.)

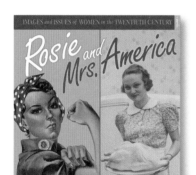

Although I felt we overpaid, this acquisition has worked out well. We added titles and created work for IGI and Muscle Bound. TFCB also put us into the upper grades market where we needed help and new product.

GRAPHIC UNIVERSE

One of the exciting things about publishing is that it's always changing. Take comic books. I read them as a kid just for fun. These days comic books—or graphic novels, as some call them—are a burgeoning slice of the children's publishing pie. We wanted to test the waters of this new area and started publishing classic myths and legends in comic-book–style in 2006. We signed up artists from DC and Marvel to illustrate them and went to comic-book writers for the stories. To make a niche for them in our list, we created Graphic Universe as a separate imprint. It now publishes fiction and nonfiction and is really catching on in the marketplace.

The Hero Twins

YOU CAN'T RUN A SUCCESSFUL BUSINESS without good professionals to give you sound advice. I don't know if it was luck or coincidence, but we've been fortunate in having first-rate advisers. Our corporate attorney, Burt Weisberg, has been with us since the beginning. He has guided us through the years with advice and maneuvers

that have kept us out of trouble. He's a good friend, smart, thorough, and cautious. And did I mention he's thorough? Now his son, Brian, is giving us the same good service. By the way, Burt's father, Frank Weisberg, was the Lerner family attorney. For three generations, the Weisbergs have been giving us legal advice.

Burt Weisberg (right) *and Bob Karon*

You can't live without an accountant, and we have been dealing with the same firm for over forty-five years. Bob Karon has more clever ideas than you can shake a stick at. He's always coming up with systems to save us money. He is instrumental in our estate planning and troubleshooting. Together, we have more plans and trusts than I can comprehend, all well thought out and workable, hopefully.

Then there is Billy Siegel, six years my senior. Billy was always a bright student. After his stint in the navy during World War II, he received his PhD in psychology from the University of Minnesota. He lived on a kibbutz in Israel in the 1950s. Both of us were active labor Zionists, and Socialist ideals shaped our thinking about politics and how nations should behave. No longer are we naive Socialists, but some of these values persist in how our companies are run and how we treat employees. (By the way, my father was a Socialist. He always

> " In the late 1980s, I was working for Burt Weisberg, who had long been a legal adviser to Harry. Lerner Publications was encountering more and more copyright issues, and I was assigned the task of researching those issues. I became increasingly interested in the publishing business, and that interest, coupled with some timely referrals from Harry, launched me into a career in publishing law. "
>
> *from Lerner's literary attorney,* DAVID KOEHSER

supported Norman Thomas, the greatest idealist of the twentieth century.) Now we are realists and, for better or worse, take human nature into account. Billy and his wife, Felicia, also a psychologist, live in Jerusalem. We communicate frequently. Billy is my rational adviser and philosopher.

If you have good advisers and your personalities mesh, and if they are fair and honest, stick with them.

Jennifer Jones Won't Leave Me Alone

I'VE ALWAYS BEEN IMPRESSED with family businesses, especially if they are successful. Many immigrant families offer a model. Go into many Chinese restaurants and you'll find the dad in the kitchen and mom and kids working the tables. And restaurants are not the exception. Food markets, retail shops, and even manufacturing firms have family members working side by side.

This has been our family tradition as well. Not only my core family but most of my relatives have found that working together adds cohesion, family values, parallel interest, and bonding. Both my parents worked together in their grocery store. My brothers and their wives always worked together, whether it was at the liquor store or in the medical lab, as with Aaron and Margie. All my uncles, aunts, and cousins were joined at the hip in their business or professional pursuits.

It was my dream that my generation would do the same. It started out that way. Sharon was my teammate, and we loved it. But things change. Three of my four kids see it differently. They want to spread their wings and fly off to different pastures.

> **"** Lerner is a little older than Andersen Press, but both family companies have happily remained independent and much respected. Adam has learned the trade from his father, and I have learned from Klaus. We are delighted to see a son taking over the father's firm and building on what's already there. Long live the independents! **"**
>
> *from Lerner colleagues*
> KLAUS FLUGGE *and* SARAH PAKENHAM

My youngest, Leah, went to Barnard College in New York and stayed in New York. She was a talented designer for Liz Claiborne. She specializes in designing handbags. She frequently travels to the Far East to visit manufacturers. She is now with American Eagle Outfitters.

Number three, Danny, is in Los Angeles doing something in the motion picture business. I've lost track of his various ventures—some more successful than others. He is also acting in commercials. His most recent commercial was for Campbell soups. His wife is attending college to become a social worker.

Number two, Mia, has a master's degree in occupational therapy. But she's a stay-at-home mom of a girl and two boys. She also writes and illustrates children's books. Her husband, Raul, is a CPA for a big accounting firm. For many years, she and her family lived in Oakland, California, but they have recently returned to Minneapolis.

Here I am with my grandkids. Ariel Lerner, Adam's oldest, is sitting next to Nathan and Ruthie Posada, Mia's two oldest. I'm holding Jesse Posada, and next to me is Leo Lerner, Adam's youngest.

Only the oldest, Adam, is interested in running our companies. Adam spent many years working in publishing in New York. After my surgery in 1998, he, along with his partner Wang Ping, decided it was time to come home with their son Ariel. Leo, their other son, was born in Minneapolis not long after the move.

Our company has benefited from Adam's New York publishing experience. He doesn't look at the company as a family business but as a real corporation. He keeps saying, "We are no longer a small company." Indeed, he has transformed the company from a kibbutz into a growing corporate entity. He has taken our firm in new directions, using consultants and seeking advice from a variety of sources.

Dino-Hockey

> **"** The key to the success of Lerner is that it has managed to combine the professionalism of a large company with the friendliness and attention to detail of a small family firm. Congratulations to Harry, Adam, and Team Lerner for reaching a huge publishing milestone. **"**
>
> *from Lerner UK manager* **PAT SHEPHERD**

It was his idea to open an office in New York and to carefully examine the UK market. We now have a London presence and sell our books in the United Kingdom after modifying the text. We hope this investment will succeed.

Maybe it's inevitable, maybe it's for the best. Our company is bigger. More employees—about 200. Sales are higher—into the many millions of dollars. But are we having fun? You'll have to ask Adam and our employees that question.

Monkey with a Tool Belt

LERNER PUBLISHING GROUP'S IMPRINTS

Carolrhoda Books: *award-winning picture books, intermediate and young adult fiction, and unique nonfiction single titles*

Carolrhoda Books

ediciones Lerner: *Spanish editions of our most popular fiction and nonfiction titles*

First Avenue Editions: *high-interest fiction and nonfiction titles in paperback format for the trade market*

FIRST AVENUE EDITIONS

Graphic Universe™: *fiction and nonfiction titles with supreme graphic novel artwork and action-packed story lines*

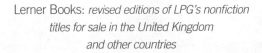

KAR-BEN
PUBLISHING

Kar-Ben Publishing: *fiction and nonfiction titles with Jewish interests*

LernerClassroom: *nonfiction materials in paperback format for the classroom market*

Lerner Books: *revised editions of LPG's nonfiction titles for sale in the United Kingdom and other countries*

Lerner Publications: *engaging photographic, series-oriented, nonfiction titles for grades K–5*

LERNER
PUBLICATIONS

MILLBROOK PRESS

Millbrook Press: *fascinating illustrated nonfiction titles and single title photo books for grades K–5*

Twenty-First Century Books: *top-quality nonfiction titles for middle school and high school readers*

T	F
C	B

MORE QUOTES FROM FRIENDS AND ASSOCIATES

Adam and I, our family, and the staff of Lerner Publishing Group are grateful to all those friends and colleagues who offered us congratulations on our fifty years in publishing. The following is a potpourri of their well wishes in no particular order.

Lerner's commitment to providing quality reading material to children is second to none. Their book donations to area preschoolers at the annual Legislative Early Childhood Read-a-Thon at the State Capitol is just one example of their uncompromising mission to help every child reach his or her full potential. Congratulations on a successful 50 years!

State Representative Nora Slawik
chair, House Early Childhood Learning Finance Division

As vice chair of the annual Legislative Early Childhood Read-a-Thon at the State Capitol, I want to thank Lerner Publishing Group for their commitment to providing quality reading material to children. The generous donation of books to area preschoolers at our annual Read-a-Thon at the State Capitol assists us in making the event a success and underscoring our message about the important role books and reading play in the development of each child as a successful learner.

The joy of sharing the imagined world created by a good story with a child is one of the great pleasures of life. It gives me great pleasure to offer Lerner Publishing Group congratulations on a successful 50 years!

State Representative David Bly
vice chair, House Early Childhood Learning Finance Division

After working with Adam Lerner for four years, I believe Adam is crazy. Crazy enough to ask why when others don't. Crazy enough to demand more, while offering the right blend of support, guidance, and freedom. The results show Adam's leadership is exactly what Lerner needs today . . . and tomorrow.

T. J. Tedesco
Grow Sales, Inc.

It must have been over twenty years ago when I first met Harry and it was a time when big international companies—managed by executives with big egos but with little knowledge of children's publishing—began to acquire smaller businesses and to dominate the market. How different was Harry—smarter, decent, modest, and humorous—from the people who wooed and pursued him. I like to think that while I too was part of the hunt, Harry knew I was never quite like the rest of the pack and opened the gate to our long-time friendship. Thanks Harry!

Thomas Sand
senior vice president, Health Communications Inc.
(publishers of the Chicken Soup series)

I knew I would enjoy writing books for a publisher in a city as cool as Minneapolis, but I didn't know what a pleasure it would be to work with Harry and Adam. Thanks for all you do to make such wonderful books. Congratulations on 50 years!

Laurie Friedman
author, the Mallory series

Campfire Mallory

Ever since my 2005 trip to Minneapolis as the brand new editor in chief of PW, *I've enjoyed a special relationship with both Lerners. They didn't know me from, um, Adam, but they've always been warm and supportive—and frank and opinionated—about all things* PW. *One of my proudest possessions is a letter pinned to my office bulletin board. Harry sent it to me after I appeared on* The Today Show. *"Move over, Katie Couric," it says. " You're about to lose your job to Sara Nelson. You were terrific on NBC." Thank you, Adam and Harry, for your belief in me, your support, and your friendship.*

Sara Nelson
former editor in chief, Publishers Weekly

Water for One, Water for Everyone

Adam has done a remarkable job—at an especially young age—of building upon Harry's enormous legacy and launching Lerner Publishing Group into the twenty-first century. He is quickly creating a legacy of his own. We feel privileged to know him and to call him our dear friend. Congratulations to the Lerner family on 50 wonderful years. Go Kar-Ben!

Pamela S. White and R. Sid Albert
Random House executives

I first met Adam Lerner when I was the paperback reprint buyer for Puffin and he was selling sub rights. I admired his forging his own path in New York publishing; I appreciated the fact that he was direct and didn't play games. We did good business and it was, as the cliché goes, a pleasure. What was even more of a pleasure was the unexpected Adam. I remember various meals, including dim sum (where I got stuck with chicken feet); Veselka, with his family (although he moved before I could be a babysitter); some "ethnic" meal at a food court at an ALA (where we were joined by the cosmopolitan Peter Sís). Although we don't do business now, I am honored to count him as a friend.

Sharyn November
senior editor, Viking Children's Books

I started to work as Harry's CPA along with Harvey Orenstein in 1971. At that time, I became very close to Harry, Sharon, and all of the very young Lerner children. Over the 25 years that I was Harry's adviser, I looked forward to all of my meetings with Harry. Why? Not just to give advice but to get advice. Harry is one of the brightest business people I have ever known and have had the pleasure of working with. My congratulations to Harry, Sandy, Adam, and the entire family for their unequaled success in the publishing industry.

Barry Rubin

Fast 'n' Snappy

To Adam and team from your distributors Down Under:

Lerner Publishing Group has nailed it! Cosmopolitan content, stylish design, international marketing...Kiwis love Lerner! Congratulations on 50 years of quality publishing.

John Mansbridge
former managing director, South Pacific Book Distributors Limited
Auckland, New Zealand

As a customer and cousin of Harry and Adam, it has been my pleasure to know them and admire the business they have built. My first business recollection of Lerner Publishing Group was having dinner with Harry and Sharon at an IRA over 25 years ago. Adam and I have continued this annual tradition and both of us look forward to many more IRAs together. I wish to extend my warm congratulations on Lerner's 50th Anniversary and toast this celebratory milestone.

Dennis K. Goldman
president, ETA Cuisenaire
(publisher of educational manipulatives)

Adam worked for me in the Rights Department in the 1980s (I think) at Macmillan. I also think it may have been his first publishing job. He was a hard worker, very professional—even then, and a great addition to the department. I was sorry when he left for FSG, but I think it was a good move for him, and he has just continued to excel and to contribute to the best in children's publishing.

Pat Buckley
retired vice president and subrights director
Harper Children's Books

Christmas Is Coming

Here I am with the U.S. ambassador to Uganda, Jimmy J. Kolker, at a Books for Africa event on September 1, 2005.

Harry Lerner must be acknowledged for the support of the organization BOOKS FOR AFRICA that I started in 1988. Well over 20 million books have been sent to nearly 40 countries in Africa. I think it's safe to say that, without Harry's unflagging support, we would not be where we are today.

It was a struggle in the early years, and Harry's support and contributions of new children's books made all the difference. I know the Lerners to be supporters of many philanthropic causes, but their interest in Africa has been apparent in many different ways. It is not always easy to find support for international causes locally, but we know they can be counted on. May the firm thrive for another fifty years!

All best wishes,

Thomas E. and Zantha LaFon Warth

Apart from his abundant creative energies he has invested in his business, what I have come to learn about Harry Lerner since beginning my volunteer work to document the Minnesota book world for the Minnesota Historical Society is that Harry is a veritable, walking encyclopedia of Minnesota publishing and book world history.

Julian G. Plante, Ph.D.
founding director emeritus
Hill Monastic Manuscript Library
Saint John's Abbey and University
Collegeville, Minnesota

Many, many congratulations to Harry, Adam, and the staff at Lerner both past and present for this milestone of achievement. Fifty years in business demonstrates tenacity, integrity, superb character, grit, survival, and drive for success. Well done everyone. Here's to the next fifty years!

Claire Thompson
marketing director, Turnaround Publisher Services Ltd.
London, England

It has been an honor and privilege being your insurance agent over the years. Harry and Adam: continue carrying the torch in your capable, winning ways!

Daniel Ribnick

Best Wishes to Harry and Adam for fifty years of great publishing. From Harry's origins as the publisher of the definitive guide for GIs attempting to import a Volkswagen Beetle into the States to Adam's own innovations across a wide range of subjects, one will expect to see the Lerner list morph and grow in new and exciting ways.

Roger Rosen
president, The Rosen Publishing Group, Inc.

Like so many others, I started my publishing career by attending Harry Lerner's School of Book. He provided an education in making books start to finish. In those days, we still used keylines, dyluxes, and color keys—and the building was heated with coal! Eventually we entered the digital age, about the same time we stopped getting coal deliveries.

Lee Engfer
former editor, Lerner Publishing Group

Thanks to the Sharon Lerner Scholarship, countless librarians attended American Library Association and Minnesota Library Association conferences. In fall 2008, the first annual Sharon Lerner Lecture continued the Lerner family tradition as champions of children's librarians' professional development and as partners in a variety of exciting library programs and projects.

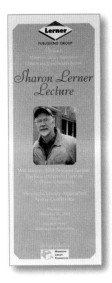

Gretchen Wronka
Youth Services and Outreach coordinator
Hennepin County Library

For many years, Harry Lerner would look over every book before it was published. I remember being called up to the very large office on the fourth floor to answer questions about my decisions. Would the title get people's attention? What did I think of the book? This turned out to be great preparation for management.

Vicki Liestman
editorial director, long-range planning, Lerner Publishing Group

Happy birthday to Lerner Publishing Group! I had the pleasure of getting to know Adam way back when at Farrar, Straus and Giroux. Since then we've both moved back to the Midwest, and it's been exciting to see him take the reins at the family business and achieve so much success. Congratulations!

Laura Tillotson
editor, Booklist *and* Book Links

I've done only two books with Adam (and Zach), but they count among my most memorable moments as an artist and illustrator.

Stephen Gammell
Caldecott-medal-winning artist

I Know an Old Teacher

We have always had tremendous respect for both Harry and Adam and what they have done with Lerner. In addition to building and maintaining a highly admired and independent publishing program, they have always been gracious and generous colleagues and a pleasure to have in the industry.

Bruno & Dan Leone
past publishers of Greenhaven Press
current publishers of ReferencePoint Press

One can't help but admire Harry for taking the plunge, not to mention what followed—and Adam for applying his own talents and continuing the story so successfully.

John Briggs
publisher, Holiday House

Harry has always considered his publishing company a family. He has fathered countless books and has educated generations of kids. And unlike a traditional family, not once in fifty years have they talked back. It's because of Harry's warmth, vision, and personality that the company has been like a family to hundreds of employees for fifty years.

David Wexler
executive vice president of sales, Lerner Publishing Group

Lerner Publishing Group has several connections to the Kerlan Collection. Several Carolrhoda authors and illustrators, including Nancy Carlson, Laurie Friedman, Mia Posada, and Jan Schultz, have donated their original work. Former editor Elizabeth Petersen served on the Kerlan Friends board, advising especially on the Kerlan newsletter. The Lerner Foundation makes a generous annual contribution to the Kerlan Friends, who in turn use the funds to support the Kerlan Award, the newsletter, and conservation of original manuscripts and art.

I heard this story from a friend who, like myself, had been taken on a tour of Lerner Publishing Group by Harry. He took a bunch of discarded file folders out of a waste basket, folded them over, and said to a nearby Lerner staffer, "you can reuse them; this is one way this company was built."

Karen Nelson Hoyle
curator, Kerlan Collection

Harry has consistently been a strong supporter of the University of Minnesota Libraries, as well as a close personal friend. His support included offering us extensive storage space in a Lerner building before the Elmer Andersen storage caverns were built. He also offered to place the Lerner archives in this facility and served on the Libraries' capital campaign committee.

Tom Shaughnessy
university librarian (retired), University of Minnesota

I have known Harry for over forty years. While in law school in the 1960s, I worked at the family liquor store on Nicollet Island. One night when I was working at the store, Dave Lerner, Harry's older brother, told me to get in touch with Harry right away. I called him and found out that the Grove Street Apartment building, which the Lerner family had owned for decades, was about to be condemned by the Minneapolis City Council.

The building had recently had a fire, which had caused structural damage. Harry wanted to know what could be done. I made a few calls to City Hall and talked with Alderman Walter Dziedzic. He advised me that it might be possible to save the building, but only if we could find a buyer who was willing to make the necessary repairs. Within the hour, I got back to Harry.

A short time later, Harry called me back and said he had a buyer named John Kerwin who was ready to act. To save the building, we needed to produce a purchase agreement by 9:00 the next morning. Over the next twelve hours, Harry and his lawyer prepared a purchase agreement with Mr. Kerwin. At 7:30 the next morning, Harry and Mr. Kerwin executed the agreement. I rushed it to City Hall and presented it to several council members, including Alderman Dziedzic. Grove Street was reprieved! Harry rewarded me quite handsomely, as I recall.

Brian Rice

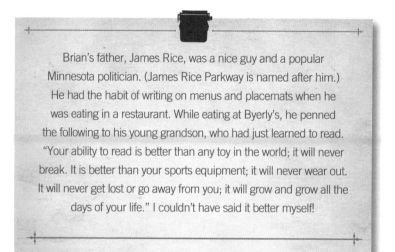

Brian's father, James Rice, was a nice guy and a popular Minnesota politician. (James Rice Parkway is named after him.) He had the habit of writing on menus and placemats when he was eating in a restaurant. While eating at Byerly's, he penned the following to his young grandson, who had just learned to read. "Your ability to read is better than any toy in the world; it will never break. It is better than your sports equipment; it will never wear out. It will never get lost or go away from you; it will grow and grow all the days of your life." I couldn't have said it better myself!

Harry has been one of the good and great Friends of the University Libraries. He served on the Friends' Board and continues to provide guidance and direction. He was instrumental in bringing the Upper Midwest Jewish Historical Archives together with the University Libraries and generously supported the partnership.

More recently, I moderated a panel at the Society for the History of Authorship, Reading, and Publishing. Adam joined University of Minnesota Press director Doug Armato and Patricia McDonald of Afton Historical Society Press in this session. What a wonderful trio of perspectives on publishing! Adam provided an insightful view of contemporary challenges of publishing, from the intricacies of off-shore production to the rise of electronic media.

Congratulations on fifty years of extraordinary leadership in publishing!

Wendy Pradt Lougee
librarian, University of Minnesota

My son Craig's first job in New York was at Macmillan in 1993. One of the young people he met there was Adam. In 1995 our books were generating subrights and permissions interest from educational publishers. I did not know much about this area of publishing. Craig suggested I call Adam, who had moved to the rights department of FSG. We met for lunch and really hit it off. Adam shared his experience willingly. At one of our future meetings, I encouraged him to return home and join the family business. In the last ten years, Lerner Publishing Group has had tremendous growth under his leadership. I am proud to say we are old friends.

Thomas Low
president, Lee & Low Books

Happy Birthday, World

Since retiring in 1995, I have marveled at the metamorphosis of Lerner Publishing Group. During periods of technological growth, changes in the world of publishing, and economic swings, Lerner has continued to lead the way in the creation of educational books. I offer the Lerner family and company my sincere congratulations on reaching their fiftieth anniversary and wish them continued success in the future.

Lloyd Schatschneider
comptroller (retired), Lerner Publishing Group

I was first introduced to the Lerner family over fifteen years ago, when I met Harry over breakfast in the Carlton Hotel in Bologna. I was immediately impressed by his candid approach and good business sense. We ran similar companies and faced similar challenges in the library market. Later on, I met Adam, who was fresh back from his time working as rights director for FSG in New York and was ready to broaden Lerner's offerings. Once again, I found we were traveling similar business paths. As is the way in publishing, both our friendship and business relationship have continued to flourish along with our businesses. We share a common vision and have common values. I am proud to count Adam as a friend and wish him and his colleagues another fifty wonderful years.

Marlene Johnson
managing director, Hachette Children's Books
London, England